TRIBAL COLLEGES

A SPECIAL REPORT

Tribal Colleges

SHAPING THE FUTURE OF NATIVE AMERICA

WITH A FOREWORD BY

ERNEST L. BOYER

THE CARNEGIE FOUNDATION FOR THE ADVANCEMENT OF TEACHING

5 IVY LANE, PRINCETON, NEW JERSEY 08540

Library of Congress Cataloging-in-Publication Data
Carnegie Foundation for the Advancement of Teaching
    Tribal colleges: shaping the future of native America / with a foreword by Ernest L. Boyer: The Carnegie Foundation for the Advancement of Teaching.
        p.   cm.
    Includes bibliographical references.
    1. Indians of North America—Education (Higher).   2. Universities and colleges—United States. I. Title.
E97.C33   1989   371.97'97—dc20   89-27994
ISBN 0-931050-36-7   CIP

Copies are available from the
PRINCETON UNIVERSITY PRESS
3175 Princeton Pike
Lawrenceville, N.J. 08648

CONTENTS

ACKNOWLEDGMENTS

THIS REPORT is primarily the work of Paul Boyer, instructor in journalism at California State University at Sacramento. He is the one who almost single-handedly designed the study, visited the campuses, and engaged tribal college presidents intimately in the project. It was Mr. Boyer whose insights and sensitivity captured both the problems and the great potential of the tribal colleges while putting the work in historical perspective. We're profoundly grateful to him for researching and writing this report and for professionally guiding the project to completion.

The Christian A. Johnson Endeavor Foundation awarded the generous grant which made the study possible. We are especially grateful to Mrs. Julie J. Kidd for her early and continuing interest in the project, and for her remarkably effective commitment and work on behalf of Native Americans. Mrs. Kidd exemplifies the kind of receptivity and connection to American Indians we envision for our society in the future.

This report also depended on the expertise of many people across the country who provided inspiration, direction, and invaluable critique.

First, we must thank the American Indian Higher Education Consortium and the twenty-seven member colleges that graciously offered their time and wisdom during the past two years. From the first days of research to the last hours of editing, the presidents, staff, faculty and students of these remarkable institutions provided essential support.

The seven colleges we visited deserve special recognition. At each there were people who took time to discuss issues, arrange meetings, and provide information. Presidents Lionel Bordeaux of Sinte Gleska College, Lowell

Amiotte of Oglala Lakota College, Gerald Monette of Turtle Mountain Community College, Janine Pease-Windy Boy of Little Big Horn College, Dean Jackson (former president) of Navajo Community College, Joseph McDonald of Salish Kootenai College, and Carlos Cordero of D-Q University, all opened their campuses to us.

We are indebted to the faculty and staff of the colleges. From them we learned about the needs of surrounding communities and about the challenges and successes of the tribal colleges. These are the people who are helping to define the future of the tribal college movement.

The time spent with students, both in class and in individual discussion, was especially meaningful. In many ways the students were the strongest advocates of the tribal colleges, both through their insights and by their very presence in these institutions. Their self-awareness and confidence made us feel hopeful for the future of Native American society.

We also gained a broader perspective on tribal issues and Native American higher education through conversations with tribal leaders, educators, and government officials on a number of the reservations. We thank them for sharing their knowledge.

In later preparation of this report, there were many people we consulted for information and critique. Steven Crum of California State University, Chico, was helpful in placing the tribal college movement in the context of history, and he critiqued early drafts of that chapter. John Forkenbrock, Tod Bedrosian, and Georgianna Tiger all helped to make sense of the federal government's support to the colleges. Schuyler Houser and Patrick Head were consulted for their knowledge of the colleges' place in a broader movement for Indian self-determination.

Many people also took the time to critique drafts of the report. We would like to thank tribal college presidents Art McDonald, Janine Pease-Windy

Boy, Jasjit Minhas, Lionel Bordeaux, Joseph McDonald, Carlos Cordero, Robert Lorence, and Gwen Hill for their comments and suggestions. Tom Allen oversaw the thoughtful analysis that came from Oglala Lakota College.

Finally, a very special thanks to Jan Hempel, who took over in the final stages of this report, editing the manuscript, checking the facts, and moving it along with great professional skill to publication. Her contribution to the project was absolutely crucial.

ERNEST L. BOYER
President
The Carnegie Foundation for
the Advancement of Teaching

FOREWORD

by Ernest L. Boyer

TWENTY YEARS AGO in Arizona, Native Americans created a new institution—the first tribally controlled college. Today twenty-four higher learning institutions, founded and controlled by Indians, are serving Native communities from Michigan to Washington State. While most of these colleges are no more than a decade old—a blink in time for higher education—they have undergone dramatic growth, expanding and gaining recognition in spite of conditions others would regard as impossible.

Researchers from The Carnegie Foundation for the Advancement of Teaching spent two years studying these remarkable institutions. We reviewed the federal government's past attempts to "educate" the Indians and discovered how, in the desert left by a long history of failed policies, the Navajos in 1968 created Navajo Community College, inspiring a movement that now offers to Native Americans a door of hope.

Viewed by the numbers alone, tribal colleges add up to only a small fraction of the total higher education picture—the equivalent perhaps of a small branch of a single state university. But using conventional yardsticks to measure these colleges misses the significance of their work. Tribally controlled colleges can be understood only in the historical context of Indian education and in the spiritual role they play in bringing renewal to their people. When viewed from these perspectives, tribal colleges assume a mission of great consequence to Native Americans and to the nation.

During the conduct of this study, we were struck by the capacity of tribal colleges to cope with resources that are painfully restricted. At almost all of the institutions, salaries are far too low, libraries are shockingly underfunded, and administrators struggle to operate with day-to-day budget constraints that other higher learning institutions would totally reject. Although a few of the colleges have accommodating campuses, many are getting by with mismatched trailers or unsuitable buildings converted from other uses. Still, faced with difficult conditions, tribal colleges have managed not only to stay alive, but also to expand their services and creatively serve their students and their communities.

These young, vital colleges, primarily two-year institutions, offer first a conventional collegiate curriculum for students who can not only complete formal degrees but also prepare themselves for transfer to four-year institutions. They enroll, as well, older students who cannot leave their home, and serve as re-entering institutions for those who may have dropped out. Tribal colleges also provide enrichment for the secondary schools that surround them.

Tribal colleges are truly *community* institutions. After years of brutal physical hardship and disorienting cultural loss, Native Americans—through the tribal college movement—are building new communities based on shared traditions. They are challenging the conditions that plague their societies and continue to threaten their survival.

For many decades American Indian reservations have been demoralized by the seemingly permanent condition of extreme poverty. In some tribal communities, unemployment reaches 80 percent. The disease of alcoholism has taken a severe toll on Indians since its introduction into their culture, and today requires the most serious immediate attention. Health care is of the most critical concern. Infant mortality rates on some of the reservations are at shocking levels—as high as double the national average. The tragedy of early death from illness or suicide has touched all members of these family-oriented communities. These crises require urgent attention, and tribal colleges are working to provide the leadership, programs, and resources to meet the challenge.

At the heart of the tribal college movement is a commitment by Native Americans to reclaim their cultural heritage. The commitment to reaffirm traditions is a driving force fed by a spirit based on shared history passed down through generations, and on common goals. Some tribes have lost much of their tradition, and feel, with a sense of urgency, that they must reclaim all they can from the past even as they confront problems of the present. The obstacles in this endeavor are enormous but, again, Indians are determined to reaffirm their heritage, and tribal colleges, through their curriculum and campus climate, are places of great promise.

As we completed our study we were forced to reflect on how the tribal college movement relates to our history, to the rest of higher education—and to the future of our country.

Well-intentioned people from the earliest white "settlers" have sought to share white civilization, through education, with the natives of this land and attempts have repeatedly been made to separate young Indian students from their culture "for their own good." The boarding school approach described in this report continues, in some places, to this very day. Throughout the years Indians have been blamed for their resistance to these efforts at assimilation, which many whites believed was essential if Native Americans were to make "progress."

But if we have learned anything from our relationship with the American Indian, it is that people cannot be torn from their cultural roots without harm. To the extent that we fail to assist Native Americans, *through their own institutions,* to reclaim their past and secure their future, we are compounding the costly errors of the past.

No one can reasonably deny that the United States has accumulated over the years large moral and legal obligations to the Indians. But past policy disasters have occurred, and continue to occur, largely because the prevailing white population for the most part can only see the relationship as a one-way street. If we would like the American Indian to benefit from what we have to give, we might begin by learning to appreciate and benefit from what the Indian has to give us.

We believe that a good place to start learning from American Indians is the tribal college, where we can learn about survival, about hope and determination in the face of extreme adversity, about renewal of community, about reclaiming the individual and the society from dependencies of all sorts, and about creatively connecting education to the larger world. Clearly American society as a whole has a great deal to gain by supporting the tribal college movement—and learning from the first Americans.

It is in this spirit that we make our recommendations. The need of the colleges for more financial support is a vital part of what we found, but it is only a part. Equally important is the need for more connections between the larger American society and the Native American communities through support of the tribal colleges. Native Americans have laid the groundwork by dint of sheer determination and conviction. They are on the threshold of a new era. Building on this remarkable beginning will serve us all.

Tribal Colleges: A New Era

THE STORY OF the Native American experience has been described, almost always, in the language of despair. Indian life is filled with images of poverty, and government policy has consistently been called a failure. We often speak of "the plight of the Indians" and conclude with resignation that little can be done. But there is in fact a lot that can be done. We report here on some of the great beginnings that have been accomplished by Indians for themselves, and offer recommendations for support that should be offered to help assure their continued growth.

At the heart of the spirit of renewal among Indians is a network of Native American colleges providing education and community service in a climate of self-determination. Although the oldest "tribal college" was started just two decades ago, these fledgling institutions are creatively changing the educational and social landscape of the reservations.

Learning is the key. Native Americans are now being educated in large numbers—and they are being heard. They are challenging the economic stagnation in reservation communities, and they are aggressively confronting the devastating impact of alcoholism and drug abuse. Of equal importance, they are reaffirming tribal traditions that were slipping away.

The general population's perception is rooted in some reality. Indian reservations are isolated, chronically neglected places that have benefited little from the nation's wealth. Unemployment and alcoholism are depressingly persistent problems in these forgotten regions, and statistics on life expectancy, infant mortality, family income and educational opportunities among Native Americans parallel those of Third World countries.

But after years of physical hardship and cultural neglect, Indians themselves are again gaining the confidence and skills needed to lead their nations. A new mood of optimism and self-respect among native people is beginning to emerge.

The first tribal college opened in 1968 on the Navajo Reservation in northern Arizona. As Navajos began to assert their rights more aggressively, there was frustration that few tribal members had the skills needed to provide leadership for an Indian nation of more than a hundred thousand people. Leaders recognized higher education as a key to self-determination.

Twenty years later, Navajo Community College has over one thousand students enrolled on a sprawling modern campus on the high desert plateau west of Gallup, New Mexico. Located in the geographic center of the reservation, the college also remains at the heart of the Navajo people's efforts to control their own destinies.

Today, there are twenty-four tribally controlled colleges scattered in eleven Western and Midwestern states—from California to Michigan, and from Arizona to North Dakota. Together these institutions have a full-time equivalent enrollment of more than 4,400 students and serve over 10,000 Native American individuals.

The Carnegie Foundation spent two years studying these colleges and the ideas they represent. During our visits, we were greatly impressed by the educational opportunities tribal colleges provide and by the pride these institutions inspire in both students and tribal members. In their cultural rootedness and powerfully considered purposes, tribal colleges are unparalleled.

At the same time, the challenges these institutions confront cannot be overstated. A typical tribal college necessarily charges low tuition but lacks a tax base to support the full education costs. Meanwhile, the limited federal support these colleges receive—the backbone of their funding—fails to keep pace with their enrollment growth.

Classes at tribal colleges frequently are held in shabby buildings, even trailers, and students often use books and laboratory equipment that are embarrassingly obsolete. At the same time, the colleges are educating many first-generation students who usually have important but competing obligations to their families and local communities.

Tribal colleges also offer vital community services—family counseling, alcohol abuse programs and job training—with little financial or administrative support. Successful programs frequently end abruptly because of budget cuts.

Considering the enormously difficult conditions tribal colleges endure, with resources most collegiate institutions would find unacceptably restrictive, their impact is remarkable. It became unmistakably clear during our visits that, even as they struggle to fulfill their urgent mandates, tribal colleges are crucial to the future of Native Americans, and of our nation.

First, tribal colleges establish a learning environment that encourages participation by and builds self-confidence in students who have come to view failure as the norm. The attrition rate among Indian students, at both the school and college levels, greatly exceeds the rate for white students.[1] Isolated by distance and culture, many have come to accept that they cannot complete school. College seems to many Native Americans an impossible dream. Tribal colleges offer hope in this climate of despair.

Most of these colleges offer tutoring programs that build basic skills and have active counseling programs for their students. At one tribal college, for example, the president even takes time to go to the homes of students who start missing classes. Education is viewed as a door of opportunity, not a cul-de-sac for failure.

Second, tribal colleges celebrate and help sustain the rich Native American traditions. For many Americans, Indian culture is little more than images of teepees, peace pipes, and brightly colored rugs. But in many reservation communities, traditional cultural values remain a vital part of the social fabric. Tribal languages are still spoken, and traditional arts and crafts and spiritual beliefs are respected.

While non-Indian schools and colleges have long ignored Indian culture, tribal colleges view it as their curricular center. They argue that it is through a reconnection to these long-standing cultural skills and beliefs that Indians can build a strong self-image and participate, with confidence, in the dominant society. Each of the tribal colleges offers courses, sometimes taught by tribal elders, in native language, story-telling history, and arts.

Beyond the classroom, traditional values also are embedded in the very spirit of these institutions. Cooperation is valued, for example. Respect for elders is encouraged. Differing ideas about how time should be managed and how people should interact with each other are understood and accepted. In mainstream institutions, Indians find their own values undermined; tribal colleges reinforce the values of the Indian culture.

Third, tribal colleges provide essential services that enrich the communities surrounding them. These colleges are, in the truest sense, *community* institutions. Located on reservations, nearly all colleges offer social and economic programs for tribal advancement. Some offer adult education, including literacy tutoring, high school equivalency programs, and vocational training. Others work cooperatively with local business and industries to build a stronger economic base. At one college, seminars for tribal

4

leaders have been held to address a variety of leadership and management issues. Administrators of this college have also successfully challenged, in court, discrimination against tribal members by the state in drawing voting district lines and by the county in its hiring practices.

Fourth, the colleges are often centers for research and scholarship. Several have established cooperative programs with state universities to conduct scientific research, while others sponsor seminars and studies about economic development needs.

To cite just one measure of achievement, twelve of the colleges are now fully accredited and eight others are now candidates for accreditation, a remarkable feat considering how young the colleges are and how thoroughly they have been scrutinized by the regional accrediting agencies, as well as by federal administrators and auditors. Within a three-year period, all the colleges were audited by the General Accounting Office and, at one point, one fully accredited college had more outside evaluators than staff on campus. Clearly, tribal colleges are not marginal institutions that have been "given a break."

These institutions have taken on a breathtaking array of responsibilities. As they move beyond their infancy, successes are now clearly visible; their value is well documented. But recognition and acceptance happened *despite* the federal government's benign neglect and a lack of national awareness of their merits.

Relative to enrollment, federal support to tribal colleges has, in fact, declined for nearly a decade. Private support, while expanding, cannot fill the gap. Even with a twenty-year history, the tribal colleges are known to only a few Americans, and they continue to be ignored by much of the higher education community.

5

Tribal colleges have moved through a painful period in which they have struggled to secure even minimum support. We believe, however, that a decade of unprecedented opportunity is emerging, one in which tribally controlled colleges can achieve maturity and bring vitality to the reservations. America must affirm and aggressively support these institutions as they prepare to meet, in a new century, the needs of their communities.

A History of Mis-education

AMERICA'S MAINSTREAM COLLEGES have enrolled Indians for over 350 years. From the time of the first English settlement, Native Americans have been encouraged to participate in this ritual of Western civilization. But the goal was almost always assimilation, seldom the enhancement of the Indian students or the well-being of their tribes.

In 1619, the fragile Jamestown settlement in Virginia was only tenuously rooted in the New World. Still, at the first Assembly of Burgesses, "workmen of all sorts" were urged to contribute their skills "for the erecting of [a] university and college."[1] When the East India School opened its doors in 1621, included in the first student body were Indian children from the local tribe.

A commentator of the time put the purposes for enrolling Indians this way: "It would be proper to draw the best disposed among the Indians to converse and labor with our people for a convenient reward that they might not only learn a civil way of life, but be brought to a knowledge of religion and become instruments in the conversion of their countrymen."[2]

While the East India School's charter called for the education of Indian boys "in the first elements of literature," missionary work was a more urgent motivation. It was expected that Indian students would embrace the Christian faith and carry on "the work of conversion" after graduation. These hopes were soon dashed, however, when in 1622 the superintendent of the East India School and some residents were killed during an Indian uprising. The fledgling college closed.

Harvard College, founded in 1636, listed among its goals "the Education of the English and Indian youth of this country in knowledge and Goodness." To achieve this objective in regard to Indians, Harvard created a special college-within-a-college, for "twenty Indian pupils."[3] The response was disappointing. Few young Indians ever went to Harvard and many of those who did enter the college did not stay.

Illness and death, as well as the curriculum of Latin and the Western classics, weeded out all but the hardiest and most determined Indian scholars. Here is how one observer described the roadblocks at Harvard College: "For several of the said youth died, after they had been sundry years at learning, and made good proficiency therein. Others were disheartened and left learning, after they were almost ready for the college. And some returned to live among their countrymen."[4]

Dartmouth College was also inspired to educate and Christianize the Indians, as was the College of William and Mary. According to its charter, William and Mary was "to teach the Indian boys to read and write. . . . And especially to teach them thoroughly the catechism and the principles of the Christian religion."[5] But again, these intentions were never realized at the levels college founders had expected.

Still the American colonies tried, for more than 150 years, to incorporate the native population into the transplanted European education system. Young Indians were expected to change, and if they could not or would not meet the standards of European education, it was considered *their* failing, not the institution's. But there was little enthusiasm among Indians for English-style learning, and year after year there were few positive results.

At the time of the American Revolution, Indians were being dismissed as unwilling—or unable—to adapt to white society. With little allowance for cultural diversity, Americans began to feel pity or contempt when the natives failed to embrace Western culture. While some considered Indians "inherently equal" in a rather abstract fashion, there was among many others a scornful rejection of Native American values and beliefs.[6]

In 1785, Thomas Jefferson, reflecting perhaps the most enlightened view of the time, declared "the Indian to be in body and mind equal to the white man."[7] Yet in conversation with Indian groups sometime later, Jefferson was equally adamant in his promotion of European culture. "We shall with great pleasure," he proposed, "see your people become disposed to cultivate the earth, to raise herds of useful animals and to spin and weave, for their food and clothing. These resources are certain, they will never disappoint you, while those of hunting may fail, and expose your women and children to the miseries of hunger and cold. We will with pleasure furnish you with implements of the most necessary arts, and with persons who may instruct [you] how to make and use them."[8]

Some Indians eagerly sought to learn the trades that they believed might offer them parity with the white invaders. Most, however, argued that Jefferson's world had little to offer Indian society and that Western education was, in fact, a destructive force. Benjamin Franklin, in 1794, recorded one Indian leader's analysis of Western education's poor performance among his people:

> "But you, who are wise, must know that different Nations have different Conceptions of things; and you will therefore not take it amiss, if our ideas of this kind of Education happen not to be the same with yours. We have had some Experience of it; Several of our young people were formerly brought up at the College of the Northern Provinces; they were instructed in all your Sciences; but, when they came back to us, they were bad Runners, ignorant of every means

9

of living in the Woods, unable to bear either Cold or Hunger, knew neither how to build a Cabin, take a Deer, or kill an Enemy, spoke our Language imperfectly, were therefore neither fit for Hunters, Warriors, nor Counselors, they were totally good for nothing. We are however not the less oblig'd by your kind Offer, tho' we decline accepting it; and, to show our grateful Sense of it, if the Gentlemen of Virginia will send us a Dozen of their Sons, we will take great Care of their Education, instruct them in all we know, and make *Men* of them."[9]

As America pushed west, more and more Indian groups were physically subdued, and military leaders and civilians who followed in the wake of the American armed conquest often spoke disparagingly of what they saw in Indian communities, doubting the existence of a culture worth preserving. Prior to his becoming America's foremost landscape architect, Frederick Law Olmsted traveled through Texas and wrote his observations in detail. Visiting a group of Lipans in 1856, Olmsted reported: "Here . . . was nothing but the most miserable squalor, foul obscenity, and disgusting brutishness, if there be excepted the occasional evidence of a sly and impish keenness. We could not find even one man of dignity . . ."[10]

Harsh judgments about Indian intelligence were common. Charles Maclaren, a fellow of the Royal Society of Edinburgh, reported in 1875, for example, that American Indians "are not only averse to the restraints of education but are for the most part incapable of a continued process of reasoning on abstract subjects. Their inventive and imitative faculties appear to be of very humble capacity, nor have they the smallest taste for the arts and sciences."[11] Such comments, however, only serve to demonstrate the profound ignorance of Anglo commentators. Rarely were the skills and knowledge of Native American groups recognized and reported.

10

In the aftermath of military struggles in the western lands during the early post–Civil War period, treaties were signed with the various tribes. The immediate goal was to give white settlers more land to control. But each document contained provisions intended both to subdue the Indians and transform their cultures. Often grants were provided through these documents for the promotion of education and for the introduction of white civilization through such artifacts as mills and blacksmith shops.

Again promises were broken. Few of the educational commitments were fulfilled. Some schools were built, but they were small and scattered. Since the *public* effort to educate the Indian children remained erratic and largely unsuccessful, the responsibility shifted largely to missionary groups. The Civilization Act of 1816 gave money for religious groups to promote Christianization and education among Indian tribes. While leadership differed, the assimilation goals of both the public and private schools were much the same.

As Indians were driven farther and farther from population centers, "reformers" began to call for complete integration of Indians into American culture. On the belief that Native Americans could best be served through their full absorption into the white world, schools were founded to provide a necessary bridge. In this era, publicly supported, off-reservation boarding schools were started. It was believed that children could be more easily educated if they were removed from their families and communities.

Richard Henry Pratt, an Army captain, was the most enthusiastic champion of this new educational philosophy. Granted use of an old army barracks in Pennsylvania by Congress, Pratt founded, in 1879, the Carlisle Indian School, where he gathered together two hundred Indian children and young adults from different Western tribes for academic and vocational learning, as well as socialization, built around a rigid daily schedule that

11

included considerable physical labor. Pratt envisioned enough "Carlisles" to accommodate *all* Indian children. It was, he believed, the only way to make "real Americans" out of Indians. Such a view was generally seen as impractical, but the philosophical underpinnings were, nonetheless, consistent with the best hopes of policymakers.

Advocating complete submersion in white culture, Pratt made every effort at Carlisle to separate Indian students from their own heritage, including language. Use of English was mandatory at all times and violators were punished. Traditional Indian dress was not acceptable. Long hair on men was cut. Any evidence of attachment by students to their own cultures was viewed as an act of defiance. In his memoirs, Pratt noted, "I believe in immersing the Indians in our civilization and when we get them under, holding them there until they are thoroughly soaked."[12]

Religion continued to be a powerful force in Indian education efforts. Elaine Eastman, a sympathetic biographer of Pratt, noted in this regard: "Character-building through work and other wholesome discipline was reinforced by simple, nonsectarian religious teaching, the girls in small groups by members of the school faculty, the boys dispatched on Sunday mornings to different churches in town for wider experience."[13]

Carlisle and similar boarding schools were viewed by their advocates as institutions of hope and inspiration. By the turn of the century, there were twenty-five boarding schools, and amid the general ignorance and fear found in the white population, leaders at these schools argued that Native Americans deserved academic opportunity and could succeed, even excel, if motivated. Pratt believed that, with kind but firm guidance, "the mantle of citizenship will fit and sit comfortably upon [the American Indian]."[14]

Pratt's belief in the capacity of Indians to learn was, for that era, an enlightened vision. But within a few decades of Carlisle's founding, the failure of assimilation was clear. Here, as elsewhere, living conditions and the quality of education were often very poor. Discipline was harsh, and with limited federal funding, much of each student's day involved manual labor needed just to maintain the campus. Pratt called the work "character-building." In 1915, however, the Commissioner of Indian Affairs admitted that without the free labor of their students the schools could not be maintained, as Congress had not appropriated enough money for that purpose.

The missionary boarding schools were similar to Carlisle in their approach to education. One young woman, a student at a Catholic mission school in western Montana during this era, recalled the structured daily routine:

> With breakfast over, the long line of girls marched to the recreation room. From here each departed to perform her daily task. This duty was called "our charge." Depending on our age, it could be dusting the schoolrooms, or tearfully trying to build the fire with green cottonwood. There were long, cold corridors to sweep; wide, winding stairways to polish; parlors to arrange and a recreation room to put in order. . . . These and many other undertakings were accomplished before the school bell rang at nine o'clock.[15]

One gets the impression that this school was more concerned about hygiene than education.

Dropout rates at Indian boarding schools were always high—young students, to stay in school, had to be away from home and family for long periods of time. For the minority that did graduate, there was little chance for advancement either on or off the reservation. The Indians who passed through these schools were no longer considered a part of their tribal culture. Further, there were few jobs, since most graduates were trained for work not

13

available on reservations. The complaints recorded years before by Benjamin Franklin remained unresolved.

The curriculum at both the boarding and the reservation schools stressed basic work skills. In the meager academic program that was offered, the rich heritage of the various tribes was rarely mentioned. In 1915, a new federal curriculum was proposed for all government-run Indian schools. It allotted time for English, arithmetic, geology, hygiene, and even breathing exercises, but included only one reference to Native American culture. The introduction to the syllabus suggested that "Indian methods of hand weaving" *might* be incorporated into art lessons.[16]

There was, in the new course of study, a suggested reading list that included "Little Red Riding Hood," "The Three Bears," "Peter Rabbit," and "The Hare and the Tortoise." A full complement of Mother Goose rhymes was also recommended. Missing was any mention of the great tradition of storytelling, so much a part of Native American culture.

The history curriculum is even more revealing. Beginning with Columbus's "discovery" in 1492, the focus remained solely on the transplanted European culture, with a celebration of its spread across the continent. Wars and territorial expansion were recalled in great detail, all from the new settlers' perspective. No mention was made of the impact of the invasion from the Indians' perspective, and no reference to the heartache and upheavals of such conquests.

This distortion of history was no accident. Thomas Morgan, Commissioner of Indian Affairs during the late 1800s, argued strongly that educators should instill patriotism in their Native American pupils and believed that teachers should "carefully avoid any unnecessary references to the fact that they are Indians."[17]

14

To live among whites, Indians were expected to become white. In an uncompromising society, Native American students were forced to embrace European life and renounce their own culture. Such a choice left deep scars. Many students were forced into a cultural no-man's-land, where they remained torn between two worlds, suffering deeply from the schism.

The failures of the national government's policies—both educational and economic—had a profound impact on all of Indian society. "At the beginning of the twentieth century," writes historian Margaret Szasz, "the status of the Indian was not only bleak, it was hovering on the edge of disaster."[18] Unskilled and powerless, Native Americans fell into a pattern of dependency.

Rather than promoting self-sufficiency, government policies created a seemingly endless cycle of dependency and despair. The victims, once again, were blamed. Government agents, who had driven Indians to arid tracts of land and offered inappropriate training, would then return, years later, to berate their charges for becoming despondent and dependent on government rations.

Self-sufficiency was the presumed goal of federally sponsored Indian education, but quite the opposite was accomplished. According to Francis Paul Prucha, a scholar of Native American policy, "the old was destroyed, but the new was not fully accepted, leaving many Indians in a kind of limbo and fostering the spirit of dependency."[19]

This bankrupt policy reached its lowest depths of hypocrisy and inaction at the turn of the century. Signs of failure were everywhere apparent and in response, a movement for fundamental reform slowly began to take root. In 1928, there came a catalyst for action with the release of what became known as the Meriam Report. Sponsored by the privately controlled Institute for Government Research, this bold critique took a comprehensive look at Indians in American society and confirmed, in vivid language, that conditions among Native Americans had deteriorated horribly.

In the introductory chapter of his report, Lewis Meriam noted:

> An overwhelming majority of Indians are poor, even extremely poor. . . . The income of the typical Indian family is low and the earned income extremely low. . . . The number of Indians who are supporting themselves through their own efforts, according to what a white man would regard as the minimum standard of health and decency, is extremely small. . . . Many of them are living on lands from which a trained and experienced white man could scarcely wrest a reasonable living.[20]

Two days after the report's release, a *New York Times* editorial agreed with the document's central argument, lamenting that ". . . our relations with the Indians during the last few decades have been characterized by good intentions without a sympathetic understanding of the Indian's needs, and that we have done little of a practical nature to help them adapt themselves to the conditions which they have to face."[21]

In its critique of Indian education, the Meriam Report focused on government-run boarding schools. Although by the 1920s boarding schools provided for the education of only about one quarter of the total Indian student population, the report focused on these institutions as symbols of the need for fundamental change. The study offered detailed evidence of mismanagement and physical abuse at these institutions, reporting that, at times, students were provided a diet that guaranteed only slow starvation. Military order, harsh discipline, and poorly trained teachers also were criticized.

Looking at the curriculum, the Meriam Report charged that government-run schools were not providing skills relevant to Indians. It was argued that curricula in these schools were too uniform, that they stressed only white culture and ignored the many cultural differences found among tribes. The report argued that "Indian tribes and individual Indians within the tribes vary so greatly that standard content and methods of education would be worse than futile."[22]

The report also attacked the heavy emphasis on vocational training that often closed rather than opened doors. The trades offered were in areas with little chance for employment, and the detachment of the training from Indian culture left students isolated from their heritage. The addition of Indian culture into the curricula would, the report argued, reduce this unnecessary separation.

The Meriam Report had instant impact. Six months after its release, the *New York Times* summarized the new mood. "It is time to consider a question of principle," the editorial began. "Is it right to continue the policy of trying to de-Indianize the Indians and make white men out of them?"[23] Within five years, twelve boarding schools had closed or changed to daytime schools, and some schools had introduced programs encouraging Indians themselves to teach native arts.

Following the election of Franklin Roosevelt in 1932, the pace of reform quickened. John Collier was appointed Commissioner of Indian Affairs. A scholar of Indian culture and advocate of community-based education, Collier was determined to shape government policies on the basis of *Indian* needs, not on the basis of what whites wanted Indians to become. Under his leadership, the next twelve years brought sweeping and historic changes in Indian education policy.

First, Collier redefined the federal government's relationship with Native Americans. He argued that "Indian societies, whether ancient, regenerated or created anew, must be given status, responsibility and power."[24] In response to this fresh thought, the Indian Reorganization Act was passed by Congress in 1934. Designed to reverse the devastation of long-standing policy, the new legislation focused on safeguarding Native American sovereignty. Among the four key provisions in the bill were commitments to Indian self-government, the consolidation of Indian land holdings, economic development on the reservations, and support for cultural pluralism—the restoration of cultural traditions. Self-determination, for the first time, became a centerpiece of Indian policy.

In the new legislation, education was considered crucial, but this time the goal was to free students, not suppress them. Collier wanted an education program in which Indians would gain skills to lead and also be prepared to earn a living. No longer viewed as subordinates in white society, Indians were to be empowered both to sustain their traditional culture and negotiate increasingly complex government-Indian relationships. "The grant of freedom," he argued, "must be more . . . than a remission of enslavement."[25]

Community schools became the focus of the Bureau's new perspective. No longer committed to indoctrination, these institutions were to be community service centers, offering much more than the three R's. In arid regions, for example, the drinking water and bath houses of the new schools were accessible to all. Repair shops at the schools became available for adult use, and patronage of the libraries by everyone was encouraged. In all community schools, curricula became more flexible, and courses in Indian culture were introduced. A new day had dawned.

Still, attitudes had to change. Although many educators had worked with Indian children for years, there was considerable ignorance of the culture and lack of respect for traditional beliefs. In-service training for teachers in the reservation schools was also offered, and in special summer institutes, teachers studied Indian culture and considered ways to be more responsive to student needs.

There was also a short-lived program to prepare Indians to be teachers. The need for role models—persons who could live as Indians and also appreciate the dominant culture—became a priority. But the project was canceled during World War II after having prepared only fifty Native American instructors.

The 1930s was a time of new vision and bold experimentation. Important changes were made, but the era was short. At the close of the decade, fundamental issues remained unresolved. The Depression limited the money available for innovative programs and slowed the push for overhaul and reform.

The Bureau of Indian Affairs was still unable to reassure young Indians that it was acceptable to learn about their roots, and even the enlightened schools could not, according to historian Margaret Szasz, "begin to solve the problems of adjustment for a disoriented Indian child. A course in silverwork or in Indian history did not answer the child's question: Who am I?"[26]

Further, in spite of the new enlightenment, the Indian voice was rarely heard. Policies controlling reservations and schools were still determined mostly by white administrators. Even those advocating reform apparently failed to see the irony in having outsiders design programs that sought Indian self-determination.

Barriers notwithstanding, many new insights were, in fact, achieved. It was now realized, for example, that the unique values and heritage of Indian people could not be discarded in the pursuit of assimilation. A new set of policies emerged, based on the acceptance of cultural variation and Native American self-government. While education programs did not fully meet the needs of Indian society or accept Indians as full policymaking partners, a new era had clearly begun. Collier's vision and Roosevelt's Indian New Deal are still felt today.

Reformist energy was lost as World War II shifted the priorities of the nation. Programs were cut and funding was reduced. Reflecting a man-power shortage throughout the country, the Indian Service suffered from a loss of teachers and students as both went to work elsewhere or to join the Armed Services.

Collier's resignation in 1945 marked the end of an era. It also coincided with a sharp shift in the political climate in Washington, D.C. To the surprise of tribal leaders everywhere, Congress began talking about the need to get out of the "Indian business." Such talk represented a return to efforts at assimilation that were even harsher than those which had prevailed before the New Deal reform. A number of tribes were actually terminated, legal jurisdiction of Indian reservations was transferred to states, and various federal services were withdrawn.

The consequences were disastrous. Economic conditions worsened for Native Americans. Unemployment rates shot up and the educational advancement begun under the Indian Reorganization Act faltered. The federal government organized a large relocation program, moving some 125,000 unemployed Indians from reservations to large urban centers. The promises were expansive—good housing, education, a good job, and prosperity—but the reality was devastating. Job training was inadequate, economic conditions were poor, and little was done to address the isolation and the discrimination the transported Indians endured. For many, it was yet another "trail of tears."

During this post–World War II period, Indian education at government-run schools remained sensitive to Native American beliefs, but most schools were now focused uncompromisingly on one-way integration. As late as 1952, the federal commissioner in the Bureau of Indian Affairs insisted that the ultimate objective of Indian education must be "complete integration into the American way of life."

20

But the mood of the entire nation was again changing. During the 1950s and 1960s, the civil rights movement promoted a deeper understanding of Native American concerns. The Civil Rights Act, especially, ushered in legislation to aid underserved groups.

Finally, opportunity was no longer seen as merely a gift, but was held as a right, available to all. By 1965, the Higher Education Act focused on much-needed aid to students and to developing institutions, setting the stage for greater Indian participation in higher education.

This time Native Americans demanded to be heard. Assimilation arguments now confronted sharp and persistent opposition from Indian groups. The message finally got across, and in 1968 President Richard Nixon decreed that the "right of self-determination of the Indian people will be respected and their participation in planning their own destiny will actively be encouraged."

For the first time, many tribes began to voice their own vision of the future. Limited educational advancement would no longer be tolerated. Vocational training was not adequate. There was an urgent need for leadership among Native Americans, and Indian-controlled, quality education was essential. The stage was set for the founding of the first tribal college.

Tribal Colleges: A Study of Survival

IN 1911, an Indian named August Breuninger proposed the creation of an Indian university that would focus on Native American culture and be connected to an Indian museum.[1] In a letter outlining his proposal, Breuninger argued that such an institution would both create opportunity for Indians and demonstrate the vitality of Indian culture:

> A University for Indians is the greatest step that we educated Indians could make in uniting our people. . . . It would eliminate the general conception—that an Indian consists of only feathers and paint. It would single us out—as REALLY PROGRESSIVE INDIANS. It would give us a better influence with the rising generation, by setting out our character in such a conspicuous manner as to be . . . observed and imitated by them.[2]

Advocates of an Indian-controlled college were not looking to retreat from the modern world; rather, the goal was to foster a more successful path for native people toward participation as equals in the larger American society. It was not surprising, though, that the strict assimilationists of the period opposed such efforts. For example, Richard Pratt, head of the Carlisle Indian School, was convinced that Indian-controlled education would work against the integration of Indians into American society. In his eyes Indian culture was, by definition, a hindrance to advancement.

Against this prevailing attitude, proposals for native colleges continued to be made periodically for another half century, with little result. It was not until 1968 that the politics, philosophical arguments and pragmatic need all came together on the Navajo Reservation, and the first tribally controlled college was at last founded.

The impetus for the creation of Navajo Community College came directly from the Indians themselves. The college was established with the aid of various grants, and two years later received support from Congress in the Navajo Community College Act. From this beginning followed the founding of more colleges.

Legislation during the seventies affecting the progress of Native Americans included the Indian Financing Act of 1974, the Indian Education Acts of 1972 and 1974, the Indian Self-Determination and Education Assistance Act of 1975, the Indian Child Welfare Act of 1978, and the American Indian Religious Freedom Act of 1978. A critical piece of legislation, to which most of the later tribal colleges owe their existence, was the Tribally Controlled Community College Assistance Act of 1978.

Today there are twenty-four tribally controlled colleges across the United States. The movement quickly spread north to the plains and mountain states, where most of the colleges are found. Each of Montana's seven reservations and North Dakota's four reservations is served by an Indian-controlled college. In addition, there are a number of successful colleges that are not tribally controlled, but are administered by Native Americans and serve the needs of Indian students. Together these colleges stand out as the most significant and successful development in Indian education history. They offer a quality education within the context of Native American culture and values.

In recent years, many non-Indian colleges and universities have become more hospitable—and at least eighty-five have organized Indian studies programs.[3] Nevertheless, mainstream institutions are not able to serve well the diverse community needs that have become the special focus of tribal colleges, and the success rate of non-Indian colleges is not praiseworthy. In fact, close to 90 percent of Native Americans who enter such colleges eventually drop out.

Those who are part of Native American communities accept the fact that they do not live in isolation, but they are no longer willing to be led by the government. Instead, Native Americans want skills to determine their own future. It is within this context that tribal colleges should be viewed—not as a retreat from the dominant white society, but as a route for Indian people to reach greater equality and more constructive interchange with the larger world.

A PLACE FOR TRADITIONAL CULTURE

Tribal colleges, in sharp contrast to past federal policies, argue that there is still a central need for traditional culture. Indeed, they view traditional culture as their social and intellectual frame of reference. These institutions have demonstrated eloquently that the traditional Indian cultures, rather than being disruptive or irrelevant, are supportive and nurturing influences on Indian students.

Individuals firmly rooted in their own heritage can participate with more confidence in the complex world around them. In this way, tribal colleges are "cultural translators," according to a counselor at one Indian college. "Many students need to learn how to fit into the twentieth century and still be a Chippewa," he said.

While American education policy toward Indians has matured considerably since the first students were enrolled at Jamestown, it was not until Indians themselves became participants in determining their future that true advancement and productive interaction began. Tribal colleges are a major part of this trend and their success in the future will, in a very real way, assure the continued emergence of a dynamic and self-sustaining Indian population.

25

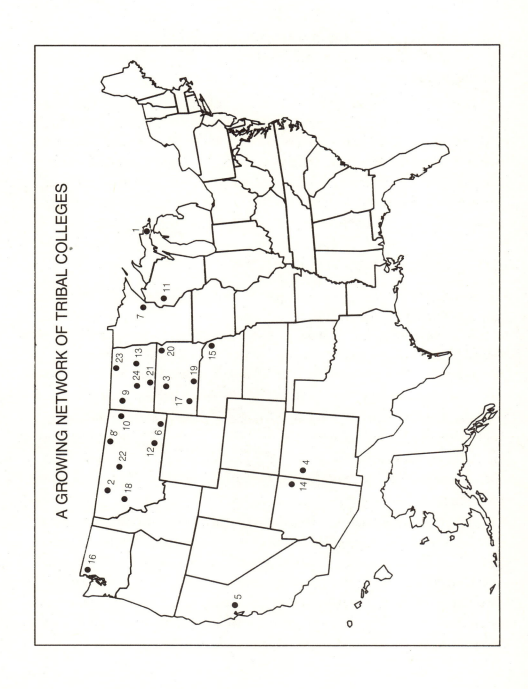

A GROWING NETWORK OF TRIBAL COLLEGES

1. Bay Mills Community College
   Brimley, Michigan

2. Blackfeet Community College
   Browning, Montana

3. Cheyenne River Community College
   Eagle Butte, South Dakota

4. Crownpoint Institute of Technology
   Crownpoint, New Mexico

5. D-Q University
   Davis, California*

6. Dull Knife Memorial College
   Lame Deer, Montana

7. Fond Du Lac Community College
   Cloquet, Minnesota

8. Fort Belknap Community College
   Harlem, Montana

9. Fort Berthold College
   New Town, North Dakota

10. Fort Peck Community College
    Poplar, Montana

11. Lac Courte Oreilles Ojibwa Community Col.
    Hayward, Wisconsin

12. Little Big Horn College
    Crow Agency, Montana

13. Little Hoop Community College
    Fort Totten, North Dakota

14. Navajo Community College
    Tsaile, Arizona

15. Nebraska Indian Community College
    Winnebago, Nebraska

16. Northwest Indian College
    Bellingham, Washington

17. Oglala Lakota College
    Kyle, South Dakota

18. Salish Kootenai College
    Pablo, Montana

19. Sinte Gleska College
    Rosebud, South Dakota

20. Sisseton-Wahpeton Community College
    Sisseton, South Dakota

21. Standing Rock College
    Fort Yates, North Dakota

22. Stone Child College
    Box Elder, Montana

23. Turtle Mountain Community College
    Belcourt, North Dakota

24. United Tribes Technical College
    Bismarck, North Dakota**

---

*Not located on a reservation.

**Does not receive funds under the Tribally Controlled Community College
Assistance Act; not located on a reservation.

EDUCATIONAL PHILOSOPHY AND CURRICULUM

All Indian-controlled colleges share a common goal of cultural understanding and tribal development, but there is diversity in educational philosophy from college to college and each curriculum reflects the priorities of that tribe. Each focuses on the needs of its own community and provides opportunity for students who choose to remain on the reservation.

Since all tribal colleges began as two-year institutions, most offer degrees in vocational, paraprofessional, and professional fields. Salish Kootenai's first courses, for example, focused on forestry, reflecting the dominant industry of western Montana. In time it added job-oriented programs in secretarial skills and early childhood education, responding to the need for workers in tribal offices and teachers qualified for Head Start and day care programs on the reservation.

A native studies program is a significant feature of all tribal colleges. Some students concentrate on native culture; others take courses in tribal languages, art, history, society, and politics, for personal understanding. Many colleges infuse a Native American perspective throughout the college and the curriculum. Navajo Community College, for example, has structured its campus and programs to reflect the traditional emphasis on the four compass points and the values attached to each. Turtle Mountain Community College seeks to insert an Indian perspective in all of its courses.

In addition, most colleges offer a broad curriculum that provides a firm and rigorous general education. Not merely centers of vocational education, they provide a full range of academic courses that challenges what one tribal college president called the "good with their hands syndrome."

Two of the colleges—Sinte Gleska and Oglala Lakota—have developed baccalaureate degree programs, and Sinte Gleska now has a master's degree program in education. While such a development is not likely to become universal among the tribal colleges, there is increasing interest in moving to the baccalaureate level to accommodate the genuine needs that exist.

Reflecting a deep commitment to community service, many colleges offer degrees in social service. Graduates of this program can find work with government and tribal agencies, where they benefit from being more easily accepted by the Indian community than are most non-Indians. Other job-oriented programs are offered, too, from welding to business.

All colleges contribute to tribal development and community education. Sinte Gleska, for example, has a range of services, from an alcohol-awareness program in area schools to the creation of a new policy institute working to promote greater economic development. The college also supports a literacy program that trains local volunteers to work as tutors in isolated communities. Salish Kootenai has an innovative job training program that provides free instruction in a variety of vocational fields. Standing Rock started a Montessori-type school for reservation-area children.

Northwest Indian College, also, focuses on early childhood education, offering courses on several reservations across the state of Washington. Traveling to each community in a van equipped with books and other learning resources, Northwest's faculty offers instruction and supervision to about forty day care and Head Start teachers.

Most tribal colleges have equally creative programs. Their goal is to serve students in the classroom and, with equal emphasis, the community beyond.

ENROLLMENT

Tribal college enrollments vary greatly, the number for a given college depending on the age of the institution and the size of the community it serves. None of the colleges is large. Navajo Community College remains the largest, with well over one thousand students. Oglala Lakota College in South Dakota has also grown to over a thousand. Most other institutions' students number in the hundreds, and a few of the newest and smallest have a hundred or less. Added together, Indian-controlled colleges enrolled about 4,400 full-time equivalent students in 1989. This figure represents a dramatic growth since 1981, when 1,689 students were enrolled.

The size of the movement is small when compared to American higher education as a whole, but it is important to bear in mind that most of the colleges are very young and that the communities they serve are small, often far removed from population centers.

The Navajo Nation is the largest, with over a hundred thousand tribal members, but most other tribes with community colleges have far fewer people. Salish Kootenai College has over 500 students registered on a reservation that has only 3,100 enrolled Salish and Kootenai tribal members. Little Hoop Community College, which serves a Sioux community in North Dakota, has just under three hundred students; the reservation itself has less than three thousand people.

THE STUDENTS

Most students enrolled at tribal colleges live within reservation boundaries. They tend to be considerably older than those at nontribal institutions, and most are women. Frequently, they are the first in their families to attend college. The average income, for students and their families, is far below the national average, so most require federal assistance.

Because of restricted funds, tribal colleges do not have good data-gathering procedures that would provide a full profile of their students. We found, however, that each institution has a remarkably similar story to tell. At Fort Berthold College—organized by the Mandan, Arikara and Hidatsa

30

Affiliated Tribes in North Dakota—the average student's age is 33. Single women with children dominate the enrollment.[4] The average age for students at Little Hoop Community College is twenty-nine. Ninety percent of its students are first generation college students. Most of these are single women with an average of two dependents.[5] About 35 percent of students at Standing Rock College are married and over half were unemployed the year before they enrolled. In addition, a 1983 study found that 98 percent of its students fell below Census Bureau poverty guidelines.[6] At Turtle Mountain Community College, meanwhile, 68 percent of the students are women and 85 percent of the women enrolled have children.[7] Most other colleges are variations on these themes.

Tribal colleges do not drain students away from distant non-Indian colleges. Instead, they provide an opportunity to those who frequently are unable or unwilling to leave their community. "Most do want some major improvement in their lives," said the academic dean at one college. "But they want a good job that will keep them here."

Other students come to tribal colleges after failing at a non-Indian college. Still others see tribal colleges as a valuable stepping stone between high school and a non-Indian college. While little overall information is available here, our site visits confirmed the assertion made by faculty and administrators that the tribal colleges act as a bridge between the Indian and Anglo worlds. Students looking for greater emotional and academic support can turn to a tribal college, after a negative experience elsewhere, rather than simply dropping out of higher education. Similarly, students lacking confidence can take a few classes or complete an Associate of Arts degree before transferring to a four-year, non-Indian institution.

The majority of students who enter degree programs at most tribal colleges do not complete them. Many have poor academic preparation, they feel the pressure of family obligations, and they live in communities with no tradition of formal education. These barriers are significant, and finding ways to overcome such roadblocks is a challenge all these colleges have accepted.

But it is also true that because of their unique role as community centers, tribal colleges serve a significant number of tribal members who wish to take only a few classes for personal improvement or in preparation for transfer to another college. This is a role played by community colleges nationwide.

GOVERNANCE

All tribal colleges exist as tribally chartered institutions. Most, but not all, have ensured their administrative autonomy from the politics of the tribal government through clearly divided advisory and governing boards. In all cases, though, leadership on these boards is provided principally by tribal members from the local community.

Presidents of the tribal colleges are largely Native Americans and, among the twenty-seven colleges in the American Indian Higher Education Consortium, eight of the presidents are women. In the early years the tribal college presidents were frequently people committed to tribal development but with little experience running a college. They tended to view the tribal colleges as tools to help provide economic and social parity with the Anglo community. Increasingly, presidents today are strong leaders with a background in education or administration.

FACULTY

Most faculty at tribal colleges are non-Indian. This is in contrast to the dominance of Native Americans in the administration and the student body. While tribal colleges are eager to include more Native American instructors,

32

the truth is that, because of failed policies of the past, the number of available Indian teachers is very small. Many white instructors are, however, familiar with the tribal community and sensitive to the needs of the students. Some arrive from outside the reservation, expecting to stay for only a short time. But many others call Indian Country their home and are fully accepted by the students and the larger communities.

A special group of tribal college instructors has little formal mainstream education, but is respected for its knowledge of traditional arts, history, philosophy, or language. Indian elders are often appointed as instructors in tribal studies classes or, as at Salish Kootenai College, serve as authenticators of what is taught in the native studies department. In this arrangement, instructors of Indian language and culture, along with the content of their courses, are certified by these tribally recognized experts.

There is considerable concern at tribal colleges over the high turnover rate of faculty and staff. Isolation and low pay conspire to limit the tenure of instructors, who frequently have enormous teaching loads but earn much less than their colleagues at non-Indian community colleges. The financial and, occasionally, the political pressures of the presidency work against stability in that post as well. Said one president: "Sooner or later, we all go by the sword in Indian Country."

Many colleges do, however, enjoy a stable administration, and the transition in the leadership at others has tended not to be disruptive. This has been the case, in part, as a result of frequent meetings among presidents at leadership seminars—now formalized under a policy institute. These sessions promote stability and professionalism among those who lead these institutions within the American Indian Higher Education Consortium.

In addition, cooperative programs in leadership training and faculty development have built a sense of purpose and direction. In one program, the seven Montana colleges have joined with Montana State University in a faculty development program. In just three years, a total of nineteen tribal college instructors have earned master's degrees and six have completed doctor of education programs.

PHYSICAL FACILITIES

Physical facilities at tribal colleges vary greatly from campus to campus. Navajo Community College has the largest campus, with dormitories, classrooms, and recreation facilities all surrounding a glass-walled administration building reminiscent of the traditional Navajo home, the hogan. Salish Kootenai has a small but elegant campus built in a pine grove beneath the mountains of western Montana. Space is at a premium, but offices and classrooms are comfortable and well equipped. In contrast, Oglala Lakota College operates a decentralized system on the large but sparsely populated Pine Ridge Sioux Reservation. The main administration building sits on an isolated hillside in the reservation, but most classes are held in a series of nine learning centers located on the reservation as well as at an extension center in Rapid City.

Elsewhere, colleges have made innovative use of donated space. Little Big Horn College, for example, houses its administration, library, and science department in an old tribal gym. Half a mile away, a sewage treatment plant has been turned into a science laboratory. Salish Kootenai held classes in the tribal jail in its early years, and Sinte Gleska College's administrative offices are housed in an old Bureau of Indian Affairs building that was once condemned.

Most tribal colleges are similar to Turtle Mountain Community College in the Ojibwa Cree community of Belcourt, in North Dakota. There, classes are held in a series of simple buildings constructed as money became

34

available. With a creative administration, the facilities are adequate, but President Gerald Monette admits that they are not elegant. Rarely do tribal colleges have sports facilities, student centers, or cafeterias, and money to construct such facilities is not in sight. "Getting by" is all that most tribal colleges can currently hope for.

THE NEED FOR FUNDING

The greatest challenge to tribal colleges is the persistent search for funding. Indeed the ability to secure adequate financial support will determine if several of the colleges continue to exist.

Most of the nation's community colleges are supported through local tax dollars; tribal colleges are not. Because their students live in poverty-ridden communities, tuition must be kept low. Few tribal colleges have local benefactors, and regionally based foundations are scarce in the areas where most of the colleges are found. As a result, all must look for support beyond reservation boundaries if they are to survive. They exist on a collection of grants, gifts, and federal appropriations that are unpredictable and frequently threatened. It's a frustrating pursuit, administrators said.

Most tribal colleges are located in isolated regions, away from the agencies and institutions that can offer support. Still, the colleges have been successful in finding some important financial assistance. Grants from foundations and corporations, and occasionally from state governments, play a crucial role in building college facilities and maintaining academic and vocational programs. Without such help, some colleges probably could not have survived.

Recently, the American Indian College Fund was launched. This project can, with significant foundation help, build a consortium-wide endowment. While not yet strong, the Fund promises to be an important source of operational support.

Financial support provided by the federal government is especially vital. Navajo Community College benefited from federal aid in its early years and today receives approximately $4 million annually through the Navajo Community College Act. In addition, most of the other colleges owe their very existence to the Tribally Controlled Community College Act of 1978 and its annual appropriation that has now reached $8.5 million. This funding, first sought by the older colleges in 1972, is critical for each of the tribal colleges in existence today.

The available funds are distributed according to each college's Indian student count. Only Navajo Community College is funded according to need, rather than enrollment. But support to that institution has fluctuated enormously over the years.

The impact of the tribally controlled college legislation cannot be overstated. Before the 1978 Act, there was only a handful of Indian colleges. After its passage, the number grew to twenty-four in little more than a decade. For most colleges, this aid is essential for their survival; some institutions depend on it to meet 80 percent or more of their annual operational and capital expenses.

College presidents are increasingly alarmed, however, that federal funding is not keeping up with the growth in tribal college enrollment. The total amount appropriated has climbed, but there has been a far greater growth in enrollment. This means that the amount available for each college student has substantially declined.

Congress authorized $4,000 per student in the original legislation—an authorized level that has since been increased to nearly $6,000—but the amount actually released has become only progressively smaller. In 1980, for example, $5 million in federal money was distributed under the Tribally Controlled Community College Act, providing about $3,000 per student.

This year the appropriation climbed to $8.5 million, but the amount generated for each student declined to $1,900! In effect, tribal colleges are being penalized for their own success.

Clearly, the tribal colleges face many serious challenges. The need to build a stable administration, meet the educational needs of an underserved population and secure a diverse financial base is a test for every college. But while tribal colleges work with greater uncertainty and fewer resources than most non-Indian college administrators could even imagine, the dominant mood remains one of optimism and success.

The Tribal College in Context

TRIBAL COLLEGES play an important role in their local communities. But for the potential of these institutions to be fully understood, we must place them in the context of the larger Indian movement now building.

There is a movement among Native Americans even more sweeping in its significance than the New Deal reforms. It's a movement that is resilient because it is self-directed. For the first time since becoming wards of the state 150 years ago, American Indians are building institutions and developing skills to control their *own* lives, a strategy that can, they believe, outlast Washington's shifting political winds.

The early policies of the government regarding Native Americans was rooted, as previously noted, in two false assumptions. First, it was believed that Native Americans could be removed from their own culture without harm. Indeed, it was often argued that, for their own good, Indians *must* be separated from traditional values and beliefs. Second, it was falsely assumed that the dominant society—the American government and its institutions—could unilaterally impose this separation, with education being seen as the basic instrument of change. These tragic misjudgments about how the nation should resolve "the Indian problem" produced policies of forced assimilation and paternalistic control.

After decades of misdirected effort, it is now fully acknowledged that no aspect of tribal life can or should be externally imposed. Assimilation efforts brought about a terrible destruction of Native American life, and many generations of tragedy. It is a history with few, if any, redeeming features.

Even when federal Indian policy was well-intended, success was rare. Ignorant of Indian traditions, government officials seldom responded adequately to Native American interests. Thomas Jefferson, for example, imagined Indians as gentlemen farmers, while President Eisenhower supported programs that promoted their participation in blue-collar labor. Neither of these expectations was embraced by Native Americans, who had no tradition as farmers and little urge to become mechanics.

Today's era of Indian self-determination reveals that constructive change in Indian society can occur when it is self-directed. Freed from aggressive abuse and misdirected intervention and ready to assert their cultural uniqueness in their own ways, American Indians are feeling a new spirit of opportunity and hope in many of their reservation communities. Tribal leaders are defining priorities of their own, and American Indian communities are combining, by their own choice, the values of two worlds—Indian and Anglo. While acknowledging that Indian society cannot retreat from the non-Indian culture, Native Americans also have reaffirmed those traditions and values that have sustained Indians for generations.

The emerging consensus is that you can be a lawyer and dance a pow-wow. "Cultural adaptation and change can take place if it is not forced and if there is a free interplay of ideas between cultures," according to researcher Jon Reyhner.[1] In advocating self-determination in Indian education, he declared: "Indian education must be . . . a synthesis of the congruent strengths of the dominant and tribal cultures rather than a process of erasure of the Indian culture and the transference of American culture, warts and all."

Reflecting the attitude throughout much of Indian Country, one influential tribal member of the Crow Nation in eastern Montana put the issue pointedly: "We cannot rely upon the Bureau of Indian Affairs to run our future for us. We cannot rely upon the people of Billings and we certainly cannot rely upon the state of Montana for self-government. We have to rely upon ourselves for self-government. If we can do that, I believe we have taken many steps back in time when the Crows were a great nation."

The chief of the Cherokee Nation, Wilma Mankiller, also linked the future with the past when she said, "There was a time when tribes had an awful lot of internal integrity and controlled their own destiny. We've got to figure out ways to rebuild ourselves as a group of people, and starting at the community level makes the most sense."[2]

The impact of the current Indian movement is not just philosophical or legal, illustrated by the highly publicized claim of a legal right included in several treaties between the United States and these sovereign Indian nations. The influence of the movement is also inward, touching the quality of life on the reservation, providing tangible impact on the lives of Indian people. And the reinforcement of native culture has become a crucial part of this new movement.

NATIVE CULTURE: A FORCE FOR CHANGE

Anglo leaders of the past saw Indian culture as an annoying barrier to change. Today most leaders, both within and outside Indian society, recognize that just the opposite is true. Rather than being a hindrance, traditional culture is an important force for constructive change.

But for much of white society, Indian culture still means little more than stereotypic, childhood images of feathered Indians on the warpath. Native Americans are often seen as people of the past, identified by the artifacts they left behind. And in Indian Country today—the vast empty expanses of America's West where many reservations are found—these images are exploited for the tourist trade.

Near the sprawling Navajo Reservation in Arizona, for example, interstate highway exits are lined with teepee-shaped gift shops selling Indian-style trinkets. Few visitors seem to care that Navajos never lived in teepees or that most of the products being sold are not made by Indians.

Near the Rosebud Sioux Reservation in South Dakota, a motel's billboard featured an Indian silhouette. "Make a Reservation," it urged tired travelers. But in the nearby Rosebud Sioux community, few whites recognize true Indians or care to understand their culture. "Every summer we get hundreds of people on the reservation and they are really disappointed because I don't have my feathers on, I don't ride my spotted horse, I don't live in a teepee," said Albert White Hat, an instructor at that reservation's college. " "Some visitors literally walk past us because they didn't see those things."

It is true that Indian reservations, like communities elsewhere, have changed. Most aspects of Indian life as practiced a century ago are gone, and the artifacts by which Indians are typically recognized are no longer commonly seen. Today, on the Rosebud Reservation and elsewhere, most "Pintos" and "Broncos" are cars, and tribal members dress more like cowboys than Indians. Nearly all residents live in government-built frame houses, not traditional shelters, and those not on welfare may work as secretaries, lawyers, nurses, teachers, and government administrators. Buffalo hunts are gone, although several reservations now breed and maintain small herds in captivity.

But beneath the surface, there are still the bonds of shared values and heritage that sustain communities. Increasingly Native Americans are learning this lesson of self-identity, in a true renaissance of traditional culture. Continued White Hat: "We're trying to bring a positive image back. We're telling the young people that they can be proud of who they are and what they are. They don't necessarily have to wear a feather to be an

42

Indian, but what is inside—how they look at themselves—is what's important. You know, traditions can be carried on whether you wear blue jeans or traditional costumes."

On the Turtle Mountain Reservation near the Canadian border in North Dakota, tribal members have built a series of traditional houses, ceremonial buildings and sweat lodges once used by the region's different tribes. Set in a forested region near a lake, it has become a small tourist attraction, but has also helped unite the native community and generate greater pride in their heritage.

On the Crow Reservation—which now surrounds the battlefield where General Custer was defeated—nearly all tribal members are skilled in their own language and about 87 percent speak it as their first language. Also, traditional spiritual ceremonies and arts, while not universally practiced, remain fully integrated in the society. Traditional sweat lodges sit in the backyards of many otherwise American-style reservation homes.

In western Montana, the Salish and Kootenai tribes of the united Flathead Indian Reservation each formed its own "culture committee" in the mid-1970s. Worried that old values were not being sustained, and angered by what they saw as the insensitivity of white anthropologists, these tribes started their own projects, which focus on recording oral histories, stories, and traditional beliefs of tribal elders for preservation and local distribution. Cultural events are held and courses in traditional crafts are taught. Project employees also work with the state historical society and the forest service to ensure that religious, historical, and cultural sites are not disturbed.

"Much would have been lost if the center wasn't started," said Clarence Woodcock, director of the Salish Cultural Committee, as he helped a class of local women and students learn how to make a teepee in a large sunny room filled with bolts of canvas. Speaking over the sound of sewing machines, he said that local attitudes toward traditional culture have shifted. "When I was growing up, the feeling was that it wasn't good to be Indian," he said. "This has changed."

On many reservations, traditional religion also is resurfacing. Religion in much of Indian society traditionally was seen not as a separate activity but as part of the very fabric of life. Sadly, many traditional religious ceremonies were, in the past, forcibly suppressed on reservations by missionaries and government administrators. Even during the middle of this century, traditional spiritual values were discouraged. The result was not simply a loss of faith, but a deep loss of cultural meaning and further shredding of society as a whole.

Old customs may never again become universally practiced, and Christian denominations have earned a permanent place in many communities. Still there is no longer much concern that uniquely Indian beliefs will disappear. There is, among many tribes, renewed interest in traditional expressions of faith, a recognition of their supportive influence on a tribal society.

HEALTH CARE: RESPONDING TO INDIAN BELIEFS

Health care is a grave concern throughout Indian communities today. Many reservations and regions with large Native American populations are often medically underserved. Clinics and hospitals frequently are far away or not adequately staffed. But it is in these reservation communities where the need for health care is greatest. Alcoholism alone means injury, cirrhosis of the liver, and malnutrition. There is also a much higher incidence of such diseases as diabetes and tuberculosis.

While there are few Indian physicians, a good share of them work with Native American patients where the needs are greatest. In southern California, for example, Emmett Chase is a physician at the American Indian Health Clinic and past chairman of the Association of American Indian Physicians. He works with the largely poor Native American population in greater Los Angeles. The impact of Chase's work goes beyond his willingness to work with an underserved population. He and others like him are offering care responsive to Native American beliefs about health. They incorporate, whenever possible, Indian attitudes, and involve medicine men in the care they offer. Emmett Chase notes: "I think Western medicine has something to learn from traditional Indian values," he said. "It is not just 'Take this pill.' Patients have an active role to play."

Other Indian-controlled organizations work to educate non-Indian doctors and nurses. The California Rural Indian Health Board in Sacramento, for example, offers workshops for Anglo health care practitioners interested in providing more sensitive care for their Native American patients.

In some Indian communities, problems such as alcohol and drug abuse have not been openly acknowledged, despite unavoidable evidence of their harm. On many reservations, statistics on accidents, illness, and violence set Indian nations apart from the rest of the United States. On the Rosebud Sioux Reservation, for example, the infant mortality rate is double the national average, and one study found that Indians there are ten times more likely than other Americans to die by age forty-five. The suicide rate, too, is far above the national average. There is no one in this family-oriented community who has not been touched by such a tragedy.[3]

Increasingly, however, problems *are* being addressed. On the Navajo Reservation a group of tribal members is working on community-based programs to combat alcohol and drug abuse on the reservation. On the sprawling Pine Ridge Reservation in South Dakota, the Lakota tribe now supports a network of organizations that together focus on the welfare of all its members. For example, Project Phoenix combats teenage alcoholism, while Project Recovery focuses on alcohol abuse in the adult population. In addition, the Oglala Women's Society advocates care of children and the Grey Eagle Society emphasizes respect and care for the elderly. "Some say we have too many organizations," said Tom Allen, at Oglala Lakota College. But he does not believe the number is excessive. Instead, the numbers provide evidence of the society's pressing needs and of the tribe's emerging concern for addressing these needs. For the first time in recent history, the people of Pine Ridge are looking to themselves for the most appropriate solutions.

In health care, and in other social reforms, Indians are demonstrating their ability to offer solutions to the problems in their communities and to educate non-Indians. In the end, problems are addressed and real solutions found.

ECONOMIC EMPOWERMENT

While cultural integrity is at the heart of Native American self-determination, tribal leaders also are concerned about enhancing economic opportunity within the reservation communities. This is a formidable assignment. Many reservations exist in isolated, depressed regions with no natural economic base. Poverty remains the dominant condition, and many Indian communities are among the poorest in the nation. South Dakota's Rosebud Reservation, for example, has much in common with many Third World countries. Unemployment is estimated to be about 80 percent. Similar conditions exist at the nearby Pine Ridge Reservation and on reservations elsewhere. Even in more "affluent" Indian communities, unemployment is more than 50 percent.

On many reservations, there is evidence of economic change. Some tribes of the southwest, in recent years, have benefited from the mineral wealth under their soil, while others have gained from legal settlements over treaties.

46

The most remarkable story, perhaps, is of the Penobscot and Passamaquoddy Indians of Maine, who won $81.5 million from the federal government for land taken over a 185-year period. The Indians invested the money in a variety of successful development projects, such as land, businesses and farms, and made loans available to Indians and non-Indians alike; assets have grown and living conditions improved. Already there is evidence of the long-term impact. Offered a promise of opportunity, the tribal members enrolled in the University of Maine increased in number from one in 1970 to eighty-five in just fifteen years.[4]

On the isolated Turtle Mountain Reservation in North Dakota, the tribe runs a manufacturing plant that contracts to build trailers for the military and simple automotive parts for the Ford Motor Company. The plant has become one of the largest employers on the reservation. A new, windowless metal building has recently been completed next door to the manufacturing plant. It houses a data entry firm that has 51 percent Indian control. The new company has hired twenty workers to enter information from printed computer cards into computer terminals. When fully established it is expected to employ up to a hundred workers.

The Pine Ridge Reservation was awarded a $1 million grant from the Ford Foundation to provide loans to small businesses and micro enterprises. Called the Lakota Fund, it provides up to $10,000 to tribal members interested in starting small enterprises ranging from wood-cutting operations to the sale of homemade arts and crafts. This unusual project began as an economic development conference sponsored by Oglala Lakota College's Research Institute.

"The goal is to fund areas of the economy not usually funded by banks," said Tom Allen, development officer at the reservation's college. It is hoped that by focusing on what he called this unrecognized gray market, the loan

47

program will provide opportunities for people who would otherwise be seen as high risk or not truly needy.

The Saginaw-Chippewa Tribe in Michigan controls a $10 million trust fund from the federal government. The tribe has invested the money and used the income to fund a range of community projects, including mortgages for tribal housing, loans for small business, and grants for various social service programs. It is also working to provide supplemental health care coverage to needy tribal members. Decisions on these and other projects come only after consultation with tribal members.

A Virginia-based organization, the First Nations Financial Project, has been working since 1980 to provide funding and technical assistance to tribes working on economic development. This nonprofit group provides interested tribes with training in marketing and management, and works on determining economic needs and finding needed money.

Other reservations are increasing opportunity, not by developing new industry, but by asserting greater control over existing industries in their regions. For example, local mining operations have traditionally been controlled by outside companies that contract with the tribe. Although the tribes have earned some income from these leases, it has frequently been a disproportionately small share of the profit. In the past, some tribal leaders did not have the skills and knowledge to assert their tribes' right to earn a more equitable income.

This has changed. Today, reservations have gone to court to gain control over the mineral resources on their land and to share more fully in their value.

The Crow Indians of Montana, for example, after years of litigation, were given the right to gather back taxes from a large coal mining operation on the reservation. An earlier decision confirmed the tribe's right to collect

48

needed revenue from the operation. This latter decision gave them access to $28 million that had been held in escrow pending the decision. A final decision on this case, however, is pending. It is to be decided whether the money belongs to the tribe or is a part of the Bureau of Indian Affairs trust fund.

Still, the announcement of the court's decision brought about a day of celebration. A national holiday was declared on the reservation, and there was a parade through the town of Crow Agency, followed by a series of public lectures by tribal leaders. All stressed the impact the money was expected to have on the goals of tribal sovereignty. Even economic development, it was agreed, must be judged also by its ability to strengthen self-determination.

"Finally we have the resources to obtain our goals and dreams," declared moderator Phil Beaumont. "Now we can expand and retain our culture. Tomorrow we are going to roll up our sleeves and start building the best government possible and we are going to do it without the influence of any outsiders."

Through cultural integrity, economic development, and social responsiveness, Native Americans are accepting responsibility for needs that were once either ignored or left to the federal government. Moreover, the movement, though still young, is already offering evidence that it can promote real change.

A word of caution, however: self-determination does not mean an end to the federal government's trust responsibility. Most reservations have not seen such economic transformations. Poverty remains a grim reality in most Indian communities. Often established in barren regions, most reservations do not, alone, have the resources needed for a second economy. The social and economic gains in some Indian communities must not be seen as an excuse to diminish federal and private assistance.

49

In the end, the issue is empowerment. No longer pawns, Native Americans are demonstrating that *they* should decide their own fate. This empowerment should be seen as a legal right and also as the best way to achieve greater opportunity for Native Americans. Indians themselves must determine the direction of their lives and the values they will hold as their own. Toward this end, government remains an essential partner, but no more.

Colleges That Build Communities

NATIVE AMERICANS are constructing new and more supportive communities, and tribes are working to preserve the traditional values of their cultures. The Indians, having experienced the loss of so much of what bonds a society, feel an urgency to rediscover and rebuild. Strengthening their communities depends on retrieving and preserving traditions which have come close to extinction.

The need for social bonding is deep-rooted and is one shared by all societies. Robert Bellah, in *Habits of the Heart,* explains it this way:

> If we are not entirely a mass of interchangeable fragments within an aggregate, if we are in part qualitatively distinct members of a whole, it is because there are still operating among us, with whatever difficulties, traditions that tell about the nature of the world, about the nature of society, and about who we are as a people . . . Somehow families, churches, a variety of cultural associations and, even if only in the interstices, schools and universities, do manage to communicate a form of life, a *paideia,* in the sense of growing up in a morally and intellectually intelligible world.[1]

Reflecting Bellah's vision, tribal colleges are working, not to return to the past, but to see the past as the foundation for a better present and a sounder future. In this way, reconciliation with the Native American heritage is as essential to Indian culture as an understanding of Jeffersonian thought is to Anglo-American culture.

In Indian society, as well as in the non-Indian world, education plays a central role in this search for interaction. According to Native American historian Jack Forbes, Indian-controlled colleges can fulfill the same cultural and social role in their communities that white-controlled colleges have traditionally provided in theirs:

> Native tribal and folk groups especially need their own institutions in order not merely to preserve that portion of their heritage which proves to be worthy of preservation, but also in order to develop sufficiently a degree of self-confidence, pride, and optimism . . . A Native American university can serve as an agency for helping to restore the quite obvious ability in self-management and self-realization which Indians possessed prior to the intervention of the federal government.[2]

Tribally controlled colleges, in fact, are among the most successful examples of institutions that are rebuilding shared traditions. Like their community college counterparts across the United States, tribal colleges are expected to serve the needs of both individuals and communities. What we found remarkable is that while most of these institutions have existed for only a decade or less, they already provide their tribal societies with unity and human understanding that much of American society is still seeking.

Tribally controlled colleges are, at first glance, a study in diversity. Curricula, teaching styles, and campus architecture mirror the surrounding tribal cultures, each college possessing a unique character. Some focus on general education, others emphasize vocational training. A few have campuses that would be the envy of any small rural college, while others offer classes in mismatched trailers.

52

Beyond the differences, all tribal colleges share common goals. They seek to strengthen respect for their cultural heritage, create greater social and economic opportunities for the tribe and its members, and create links to the larger American society. The watchword at Indian colleges is not simply education, but empowerment.

All tribal colleges seek first to rebuild, among students, an understanding of their heritage, and in some settings this has been a particularly challenging task. On many reservations, native beliefs, language, and traditional arts were not strong. Values once shared through a rich tradition of storytelling were not being preserved—traditional culture existed to a large degree only in textbooks, while Anglo values remained alien and unaccepted.

Tribal colleges are in the vanguard of a cultural renaissance in all of their communities. Courses in Native American culture are centerpieces. On the Sinte Gleska College campus, for example, the Lakota studies department offers classes in Sioux history, "Oral Literature," Lakota thought, and a four-course language sequence. "Today we drive cars, live in houses, and wear modern clothes," reflected Native Studies Director Albert White Hat. "But we still speak our languages and sing our songs. We are struggling to survive."

At Lac Courte Oreilles Ojibwa Community College in Wisconsin, courses in native studies include traditional clothing styles, music, and dance. Continuing education courses at Oglala Lakota College include "How to Set Up a Tipi," quillwork, and preparation of traditional Indian foods. Northwest Indian College on the northern coast of Washington State offers canoe carving, woodwork, and Indian knitting—skills unique to its tribal culture.

Even on reservations where traditional beliefs have not been so severely challenged, an emphasis on cultural integrity remains the foundation.

53

Students learn firmly that who they are and what they believe has great value. Rather than being a disorienting experience for Indian students, college represents a reinforcement of values inherent in the tribal community. Courses in Indian culture are not just an area of study. They are the bridge to tribal unity and individual pride.

Contrast this to the typical Native American experience in non-Indian-controlled institutions both in the past and now. While a handful of students has been able to overcome the cultural barriers, many have felt inferior and alienated. Researcher Danielle Sanders reported, for example, that much of what Indians find in non-Indian educational institutions "runs contrary to the social norms, self-perceptions, and expected behaviors that they have learned at home and that have been reinforced in their own cultural community."[3] Tribal colleges seek to eliminate this discontinuity between the classroom and life outside.

Gerald Slater, Vice President at the Salish Kootenai campus, puts this philosophy in practical perspective: "Many young people have a history of heavy drinking and have, in general, a lack of self-respect. But as they get more involved in traditional culture, they begin to get new self-respect. Sometimes they will quit their drinking and begin to find a life that is more meaningful for them."

Slater continued: "Forced assimilation has resulted in a lack of respect for Indians and their ways. Now people are realizing that these ways *are* good. They're different, but there is nothing wrong with them. There is a sense of pride and dignity that comes with it."

One evening, Myrna Chief Stick, a part-time instructor at Salish Kootenai, sat alone in an empty hallway while her class prepared for its final exam in Coyote stories. An important part of many Indian societies, they are used to explain natural events and offer, at the same time, essential moral

54

lessons. Students had spent the semester discussing these tales and were getting ready to act out one such story for Chief Stick.

While waiting for her students to call her back into the classroom, this teacher too spoke of the "self-respect, dignity, and honesty" that traditional culture provides. "Through the work of the tribe and the college," she said, "tribal members are starting to identify these values for themselves. In the last four or five years, people are becoming more aware than they have been in years."

The six students in the class, talking after their presentation, offered similar ideas. Wallace Shorty asserted that classes in traditional culture and language offer students insight into their own identity. "A lot of kids are Indian, but they don't know what it means to be Indian," he said. "They don't know how to go about it."

Classes in Native American culture offer a bridge to the past—and to the future, too. A student in the Coyote Stories courses said: "I think that's why I took it," she said. "A lot of our elders and a lot of our people who told these stories are now dead. Their children and grandchildren don't know them. I'd like to be able to pass them down."

What we found is that tribal colleges seek to integrate traditional values into all aspects of the institution. All activities within these colleges are expected to be connected seamlessly to the community.

At Little Big Horn College in Montana, the need for courses in traditional culture is less urgent, said President Janine Pease-Windy Boy. In this community, the tribal culture has remained strong. Instead, traditional culture is felt in how the affairs of the college are conducted. Each department tries to integrate Indian thought into its activities and much of the work is focused on adapting the curriculum to Crow values and individual needs.

This philosophy is visible in such "non-Indian" disciplines as math and science. In one of the most consistently difficult areas of study for Native American students, Little Big Horn science instructor Robert Madsen makes his curriculum accessible to students who otherwise would be prepared to fail. As a result, most tests are open book, and if a student fails, he or she is encouraged to work with Madsen and retake the exam. "I don't put a weight around their necks," he said. "If they get a *D,* they take the test over until they do *A* work." Madsen makes clear to students that they are in his class to succeed, but he is also reflecting the value placed on forgiveness in the Crow culture.

Madsen also emphasizes the relevance of his subject to the students. "A big part of what goes on in the class is not determining the composition of calcium, but learning to solve problems," he said. "The math and the science are there, but it is tied to concrete things." He stressed, however, that the focus on success does not mean that academic quality is lost. "I love giving out *A*s, but I make them earn them. This is a place where good science can happen," Madsen argued. "It is not just at Montana State University or Harvard that good science is possible."

Other colleges offer their own innovative ways to bridge the gap between Indian thought and Western education. Turtle Mountain Community College in North Dakota, for example, does not offer a separate native studies program. Instead of isolating courses in Indian thought from the rest of the curriculum, Turtle Mountain injects an Indian perspective into all of its classes and programs. In this way, Indian values and history are not just one area of possible study, but theoretically are part of all that the college does.

Indeed, a Native American perspective is expected to be included in all classes. President Gerald Monette admits that this "is easier said than done," but he believes that most classes successfully integrate an Indian perspective.

56

Social science departments at tribal colleges have been especially creative in offering traditional Indian perspectives. Emma Wilkie, one of Turtle Mountain's senior instructors, makes a deliberate effort to incorporate an Indian viewpoint in her sociology classes. Texts that treat Native Americans with respect are used and supplemented with additional books and articles that explain the Native American experience. For example, the study of family life would treat not only Anglo social structures, but also the Indian family's distinctive structure. Family trees and oral histories are popular learning tools for Wilkie.

Literature and history courses at tribal colleges are equally successful in including an Indian perspective. Even biology and geology classes have tapped into this integrative goal by including the study of local plants—including those used by early settlers—and exploring with students how the region's rolling topography was formed.

But it is clearly more difficult to find a local cultural-community connection to mathematics and the physical sciences. For some professors in these areas, the best solution has been to make the subjects as intellectually and emotionally accessible as possible. As at Turtle Mountain Community College, the Indian influence is not always noticeable in the material, but in how the material is taught.

Sister Margaret Pfeifer, a math instructor at Turtle Mountain Community College, believes students are best able to succeed when the air of academic competition is replaced by greater cooperation, a philosophy that is more in line with Indian society, where family obligations are stressed over individual advancement. Her math assignments frequently allow—even encourage—group work and mutual assistance. As a result, the quality of the classwork goes up along with retention rates, while anxiety over this traditionally stressful discipline goes down.

During our visits it became clear that Western strategies for teaching were not always the best way in Indian Country. There is no compelling reason why traditional American college techniques that emphasize competition must be used. Again it was at Turtle Mountain where an instructor told us how he had introduced cooperative learning to his accounting class. Group studying was stressed and many of the assignments were completed by students working together. Said Academic Dean Louis Dauphinais, "The students loved it." Only one of fourteen students dropped the class; many earned *A*s.

Navajo Community College has been working not only to find culturally appropriate teaching methods, but also to pattern the college's larger academic structure after Navajo beliefs. While individual courses are not being transformed, academic disciplines are being structured around the Navajo culture's traditional emphasis on the four compass directions.

The academic disciplines of religious studies, physical education, language and aesthetics all mold into a single category of attributes inherent in the east: knowledge that prepares people to make decisions. The west, meanwhile, focuses on the social well-being of the tribe. Within this category, the disciplines of sociology, history, and government fit comfortably. Other areas of study are linked to the north and south.[4]

The college itself is located in the very center of Navajo land, and the campus layout is modeled after the four directions, all within a larger circle. While not all of this symbolism may be useful to students trying to pass an algebra exam, the larger message is hard to miss. The college exists within the larger Navajo experience. It is an integral part of traditional tribal culture.

Here is how Herbert Benally, native studies director at the college put it: "The Navajo maintain that people need a sense of history to understand their immediate world and to prepare them for the future. . . . To accomplish this,

58

it is necessary only to create an education institution which will place the individual at the focus where the four great branches of Navajo knowledge meet."[5]

We were greatly impressed during our study by the distinctiveness and the vision of tribal colleges. Here, within the Indian community, there is an authentic effort to blend education and tradition. But what of the results?

At many campuses, student retention remains a problem. Many students leave long before graduation and the reasons are not difficult to find. First, there is a climate of failure surrounding education. While estimates vary from tribe to tribe, Native Americans drop out of secondary schools at significantly higher rates than all other racial and ethnic groups. It has been estimated that no more than 55 percent of Indian students graduate from high school,[6] and for those who do finish school, the level of academic preparation is often very poor.

Students therefore come to college with poor academic preparation and low self-esteem, and many come with the expectation of failure. A recent study of public high school students on the Turtle Mountain Reservation found under achievement among all students in nearly all subjects.

Overall, at least 60 percent of white students who enter college go on to complete a degree, but fewer than one-third of Indians leave with a diploma.[7] This legacy of inadequate preparation for college and lower expectations is a tremendous burden for tribal colleges.

The goal of every tribal college is to overcome these barriers. Many offer developmental classes, formal instruction in skills needed for "college life," counseling, and other supportive services. Salish Kootenai College, for example, has two full-time staff members who work with students who are slipping academically or missing class. "Sometimes it's the smallest problem that holds up student progress," President McDonald said. "A broken fan belt can keep a student from getting to school for two weeks."

Such personal attention is critical. "Students need to be where somebody knows their names," said Louis Dauphinais, academic dean at Turtle Mountain Community College. "They need support for academic angst."

Tribal college presidents told us they do not expect all students who enter to leave with a diploma. Some students arrive intending to take introductory courses before transferring elsewhere. Others take selected courses for personal enrichment, not a diploma. Another group *stops-out*, entering and leaving multiple times before completing a degree. All of these patterns parallel the experience of community colleges nationwide.

Success stories are nevertheless impressive. Problems notwithstanding, tribal colleges are beginning to bring a spirit of renewal to people in their communities. There is already a cadre of tribal college graduates who have succeeded academically and gone on for further study or found meaningful work. Before the founding of Sinte Gleska College on the Rosebud Reservation, there was only a handful of Indians working as teachers in the reservation public schools. Today there are thirty-four.[8] Other examples tell a similar story:

- On the nearby Pine Ridge Reservation, Oglala Lakota College, in recent years, has increased the number of Native American teachers from one to nearly a hundred.[9]

- Dull Knife Memorial College in Montana has, in its short history, graduated 315 certificate and associate students. In a recent survey of its graduates, the college found that half of those who completed a two-year degree went on for further study, while 70 percent of the graduates of a certificate program pursued more education. In an area of extremely high unemployment, 83 percent of all graduates were working or in

60

further study at the time of the survey and 91 percent of the certificate students were employed.[10]

- Sisseton-Wahpeton Community College in South Dakota has graduated 113 associate of arts students. A 1988 study found that 91 percent were fully employed in a four-year institution. In addition, three have earned a master's degree and one has completed a doctoral degree.[11]

- Turtle Mountain Community College found, in a 1983 survey, that 28 percent of its vocational education graduates transferred to a four-year college and, overall, more than 70 percent found jobs immediately after graduation. This is in sharp contrast to the 60-70 percent unemployment rate for the reservation.[12]

- At Standing Rock College, a total of 228 students graduated between its founding in 1976 and 1986. Moreover, while the reservation unemployment rate is about 80 percent, less than 5 percent of the college's graduates are known to be unemployed or not attending another institution of higher education.[13]

At first glance these numbers appear small. In the larger American society the impact of a few hundred college graduates is difficult to see. But on reservations with populations that range from three to eight thousand, the impact of new-found knowledge and expertise is pervasive. "The difference between these students making a contribution compared to unemployment is very significant," said Art McDonald, president of Dull Knife College.

But the benefits of tribal colleges go far beyond job placement, as important as this is. In small communities, graduates can advance all of tribal society, and their value as role models is substantial. Graduates who remain on their reservations after graduation offer the seeds of social stability, economic growth, and future leadership. "Tribal colleges are the dominant college in *their* nations," said Janine Pease-Windy Boy. "Just like Harvard works to fulfill the needs of its community, we work to fulfill the needs of ours." The tribal colleges provide more than a degree; they are the key to a healthy culture.

It must also be noted that the contribution of the colleges and their students goes far beyond the boundaries of their reservations. By offering services—ranging from day care and GED testing to alcohol counseling and literacy tutoring—tribal colleges have become a powerful, often the *most* powerful, social force in their communities. Indeed, on some reservations, the college is the only institution—government or tribal—that is examining all community needs, and working to provide real solutions. Graduates with knowledge and skills enrich all of American society. The country as a whole could learn from the tribal college's ability to connect to its society.

Tribal colleges must be judged, then, not only on the basis of those who graduate, but also on the basis of the rewards they bring. Lionel Bordeaux, president of Sinte Gleska, states the case succinctly: "Indian colleges emerged as the one vehicle that developed from within, the one that has the best chance to address all of the many issues that have not been addressed." As one example of this commitment, Sinte Gleska has a continuing literacy program, started after a 1985 survey found that 19 percent of the reservation Indians between 25 and 38 years of age lacked facility with the English language. By training local volunteers to work one-on-one with residents in isolated communities, college administrators hope to raise expectations throughout the tribe and provide evidence that academic success is possible.

Loraine Walking Bull, director of the program, says that the use of Indian volunteers is crucial. In this type of program, where tutors are often met

62

with suspicion, sensitivity to the Lakota culture is critical. Walking Bull noted: "We have to watch what we do because we can turn people off so quick. You have to have a lot of knowledge of the people and really watch what you say." Tribal colleges are able to promote this necessary sensitivity.

The Sinte Gleska campus also has an Institute on Alcohol and Substance Abuse. Although the tribe does not permit the sale of alcohol on the reservation, alcoholism afflicts a majority of the population. But despite its pervasiveness, college officials said that Sinte Gleska's Institute was the first reservation-wide outreach program. While the government-run Indian Health Service hospital has long had a treatment program, it has made no effort at education. Director Cecil White Hat believes that through direct intervention with students in the college and at the elementary and secondary school levels, the reservation community is at last recognizing alcohol's devastating impact.

Many tribal colleges also offer free preparation for the high school equivalency test—the GED exam. For the large percentage of reservation-based Indians without a high school diploma, the GED is a necessary key for entrance into college—both Indian and non-Indian controlled—as well as many government jobs and the military.

On Turtle Mountain Reservation, about 45 percent of the high school students do not finish school, but until the college started its center, the nearest GED program was over 90 miles away. With no satisfactory way to earn a diploma, many simply went without the education and remained unemployable. Today Turtle Mountain Community College has one full-time and two part-time instructors who tutor about 250 GED students a year. About 65 go on to complete the course and pass the exam. According to Director Sandy LaRocque, about 70 percent of the students are women and many are single parents. "They quit school because they got pregnant," she said. "Now that their children are older, they are coming back." For students too old to return comfortably to the public school and unable to move off the reservation, the college's program is the only acceptable option. "If there was no program, there would be no other alternative," LaRocque said.

At Oglala Lakota College, a total of 566 people were enrolled in the GED tutoring program in 1986, more than double the enrollment just three years earlier. At that college, as at others, many of those who pass the exam go on to enroll in the tribal college. At Oglala Lakota, 40 percent of its students have a GED certificate.[14]

Salish Kootenai College has also created an innovative bridge between formal education and hands-on experience. Frustrated by government regulations that made tribal members ineligible for certain federal assistance if they enrolled in college, Salish Kootenai started a work experience program as an alternate route to vocational training. Although classroom instruction is provided free of charge three days a week, the emphasis of the program is on each student's volunteer work in a tribal agency two days a week. Students are given assignments at such offices as the tribal printing plant, shoreline protection, or even a college department.

Gerald Slater, Vice President at Salish Kootenai, said there has been good success in getting students permanent paid positions after the program's completion. Some of the most important results, however, come from the feelings of accomplishment and independence. "We've had people say that this is the first time they haven't had a drink in years, that they have been sober for months because they enjoyed the opportunity to work," Slater said. "It has been stimulating for them."

Several tribal colleges are also actively working to promote economic development within their reservations. Some colleges, like Turtle Mountain,

64

work directly with local industry to train workers and strengthen productivity. Turtle Mountain Manufacturing, for example, has looked to the college for seminars on personnel management and the training of machinists. It is also helping a newly organized data entry firm by training future workers in computer use. The success of these companies, in turn, can create more jobs for future graduates.

Sinte Gleska, meanwhile, sponsors the newly established Institute for Economic Development, a policy center that is investigating realistic solutions to the economic stagnation on many reservations. And Oglala Lakota, in addition to its grant program that provides loans to Indian-run micro enterprises, has received foundation funding to study the college's own role in reducing poverty on its reservation.

Finally, Little Big Horn College has successfully challenged local discrimination in a series of lawsuits and has worked to increase opportunity for all tribal members in the process. In 1981, frustrated that Crows made up 46 percent of the county's population but rarely had an impact on regional elections, President Windy Boy and others worked to increase the number of Indians registered to vote. The number of registered voters was increased by one-half, from two thousand to three thousand.

In the subsequent election, however, Indians still were not able to exert much influence. Looking more closely at how the political system was organized, the college work-group found that state district boundaries clearly divided the reservation so as to prevent Indians from having a majority in any one region. They took the issue to court, and the judge agreed that the policy was discriminatory and ruled that the state cannot break up a homogeneous population.

Another success story involved charges of discriminatory hiring in the county. Out of two hundred county employees, only four were Indian, and while there are ninety-nine county board members, just one was a Crow. There was also testimony charging that Indian children were abused in schools. In all, Windy Boy said there were "250 prime cases" of discrimination. "The ACLU lawyers said they had never seen such abuse." The three-year process, aimed at ending discrimination in employment and in county governance practices, resulted in yet another favorable decision in 1986, something for which Windy Boy and the college are given much credit. "We have become advocates of decent and right treatment," she acknowledged.

This push for community is not unique to tribal colleges. Throughout all of American society, educational institutions are focusing on their contributions to larger communities. In a tellingly entitled report, *Building Communities: A Vision for a New Century,* prepared by the American Association of Community and Junior Colleges, this goal is given vivid definition. "Community colleges, through the building of educational and civic relationships, can help both their neighborhoods and the nation become self-renewing," the report argues. "The building of community, in its broadest and best sense, encompasses a concern for the whole, for integration and collaboration, for openness and integrity, for inclusiveness and self-renewal."[15]

In this report, tribal colleges were not held up as models for community, but they could have been. As the United States looks to rebuild a commitment to service and renewal, it could do no better than to examine the most dynamic and successful tribal colleges. Through an emphasis on traditional culture, social responsibility and economic development, these institutions have become the single most important force in their nations.

In the end, college officials insist, all of American society benefits. According to D-Q University President Carlos Cordero, the cost of keeping

Indians on welfare is much higher than the expense of putting them through college. Tribally controlled colleges produce graduates who "help resolve problems of contemporary society" and, he added, "who are going to pay taxes."

Recommendations: A Strategy for Excellence

W E APPLAUD tribal colleges for their often heroic accomplishments. The educational and cultural contributions of these institutions, often achieved under difficult conditions, is enormously impressive. Tribal colleges are giving hope to students and bringing new life to their communities. But with all of their accomplishments, tribal colleges urgently need help. They are, we believe, ready to move into an exciting new era, but reaching their full potential will require significant support from both the public and private sectors. The goal must be to assure that by the year 2000, the network of community-based tribal colleges created by Native Americans, colleges that offer quality education to their students and bring a spirit of renewal to their nations, is funded, expanded, and flourishing. Here we set forth a series of recommendations for realizing this vision.

First, we urgently recommend that the federal government adequately support tribal colleges by providing the full funding authorized by Congress. Specifically, we recommend that the $5,820 authorized per student be appropriated and that, from this point on, federal appropriations keep pace with the growth of Indian student enrollment.

The United States government has both a moral and legal obligation to respond to the needs of American Indian society. The fragmented cultures and persistent poverty in many Indian communities should not be tolerated, and increasing support for tribal colleges is an important strategy for meeting this obligation.

Federal government support for Indian higher education, for more than a decade, has focused on the Tribally Controlled Community College Assistance Act of 1978. We urge that it continue to do so, since this legislation is essential for the survival of many of the colleges. The funds provided through this act were, in fact, critical for the establishment of many of the tribal colleges during this decade. In addition, the Navajo Community College Assistance Act of 1971, the legislation supporting the college of the Navajo Nation, is of equal value to that institution.

The harsh truth is, however, that federal support has been woefully insufficient; it simply has not kept pace with the rate of growth in the tribal colleges, or with their most basic needs. In the original legislation Congress authorized $4,000 for each full-time equivalent student at tribal colleges, and later raised it to nearly $6,000, but the amount appropriated has *never* matched those figures.

Moreover, as the number of tribal colleges continues to grow and as enrollments continue to expand, the money available for each full-time equivalent student has plummeted. In 1981, for example, there was a total full-time equivalent of 1,689 Indian students enrolled in tribal colleges, each supported by $3,100. By 1989, however, the number of students had climbed steadily to 4,400 FTE, while money for each dropped to about $1,900! We urge Congress not to penalize tribal colleges for their success.

Further, there are many Indian communities across the United States that are *not* served by community colleges and where aspirations for higher education have long been muted by negative educational experiences. Congress should provide, in its appropriations, funds for new institutions without diminishing support for existing institutions.

Beyond this basic support, other federal agencies should provide discretionary grants to a wide range of tribal college programs. The Carl

Perkins Vocational Education Grant, which goes directly to states, is used by some tribal colleges to purchase equipment for vocational programs. In addition, the Library Services and Construction Act is used by tribal colleges to buy needed books and supplies for their still growing libraries. Here again, however, these funds are wholly inadequate to the need, especially in light of the fact that these institutions are just beginning and have little capital base.

Looking at the larger picture, we are concerned about the relationship between the Bureau of Indian Affairs and the Indian community, including the tribally controlled colleges. This relationship has been—and continues to be—marked by tension. The concern extends beyond the appropriation of federal funds, as the Bureau must work within the limitations of the federal budget. The Bureau has been criticized harshly both by members of Congress and the college community for not being a more positive participant in the development of tribal colleges. Programs and funding at the colleges have often been delayed because the Bureau did not establish the regulations required by the legislation. In the 1986 re-authorization hearings, for example, Senator Mark Hatfield, then chairman of the Select Committee on Indian Affairs, reported that the BIA had "failed to establish regulations, or even to publish proposed regulations for comment" on amendments voted on three years earlier.[1]

From the perspective of some tribal college presidents, this inaction and lack of support is seen as a form of political sabotage. "The BIA refuses to acknowledge, fully and sincerely, our existence," charged Sinte Gleska President Lionel Bordeaux. "It's almost as if it's the last attempt to keep us suppressed."

Indeed, throughout the Indian community, it is often argued that the Bureau thwarts the self-determination pursued in Native America and supported by the government through the 1975 Indian Self-determination

Act. Full Indian control of programs and services once held by the Bureau would, it is believed, threaten the existence of this agency. To many community leaders, it seems that the BIA is acting like most other bureaucracies—wanting to preserve its power.

This attitude toward the federal BIA office is not always held toward Bureau offices and officials at the local level. On a growing number of reservations, the local Bureau office is viewed as a benign presence, especially as the number of Indians employed in its offices grows. On Turtle Mountain Reservation, for example, all but one of its one hundred positions are filled by Native Americans. There, only the superintendent is not an Indian.

The atmosphere of cooperation that exists at the local level, however, is missing at the national level, to the detriment of the tribal colleges. We urge, therefore, that the Bureau of Indian Affairs join in a partnership of educational excellence *with* the tribal colleges. These institutions should be viewed, not as another regulatory burden, but as a crucial link between the government and the Native American communities they serve. Support for these colleges benefits all members of tribal society and helps fulfill the Bureau's responsibility to promote Indian welfare and development.

Second, we urge that the libraries, science laboratories, and classroom facilities at tribal colleges be significantly improved through federal government appropriations. We also propose that foundations help improve facilities at tribal colleges. This is an urgent need that cannot wait much longer for resolution. Typically, the reports of our foundation focus on teaching and learning, not on buildings; however, tribal colleges must be an exception. The federal legislation that supports tribal colleges includes a section authorizing funds for facilities; thus far, however, no appropriations have been made and many of these institutions are forced to carry on their work in trailers and abandoned government buildings that other colleges

72

would have hauled away or bulldozed over twenty years ago. Such poor facilities not only restrict learning, but also make a powerful statement of neglect.

Sinte Gleska College's administrative offices are representative. They are housed in a former Bureau of Indian Affairs building that was once condemned. Several miles away, outside the town of Mission, a half dozen small buildings surrounding a gravel pit parking lot house the college's main classrooms, faculty offices, and student services.

The college has been resourceful. Some buildings—such as the relatively spacious science center and the newly expanded library—were constructed from private, corporate, and government grants. Others, however, such as the native studies department, are in trailers. Two additional buildings—a fine arts studio and the bookstore—are in small frame buildings constructed by students in the building trades program.

With severely limited funding, Sinte Gleska has a functioning campus for well over five hundred students. But space and educational supplies are at a premium. Limited classrooms make scheduling difficult, there is no place for students to congregate, and no food service is provided, even though students must often travel long distances to reach the campuses. There are *no* sports facilities on campus.

Little Big Horn College, meanwhile, has some of the most unusual classroom facilities in the nation. On this campus the main college building is an old tribal gym, where several rooms to one side have been converted into administrative offices, while refurbished locker and shower rooms serve as classrooms and a science lab. In the middle, the basketball court has been made into a library for the college's 6,500 volumes.

Down the road is perhaps the most unusual science lab in academe. Given access to a sewer treatment plant, the director of the science program has turned a small room used for chemical analysis into additional laboratory space for his department. To get to class, students must walk on a narrow metal catwalk and squeeze past a two-story-high steel container. The well-insulated room does, at least, keep out the odor of the nearby sludge pond.

Some colleges have found funds to build modest yet relatively adequate facilities. Navajo Community College, for example, has comfortable campus facilities, and Oglala Lakota College's main administrative building is an elegant circular structure set on a hill on Pine Ridge Reservation, although many of its learning centers are woefully inadequate. Salish Kootenai has a much smaller campus that is stretched to its limits, but it too is attractive and well furnished.

Most colleges are jammed for space, and struggle daily to secure needed equipment and supplies. Such conditions are disgraceful. Facilities do make an important statement about the priorities we assign to our institutions, and the tribal college should stand, on every reservation, as a symbol of hope, with the space needed to serve adequately the educational needs of those enrolled.

Specifically, we recommend that the federal government appropriate funds for construction as authorized in the Tribally Controlled Community College Act so that, by the year 2000, every college has an adequate plan to fulfill its educational obligations. Many foundations have supported the construction of new buildings and the supply of materials—from books and libraries, to computers and lab equipment. This practice should be continually expanded. We do not propose spacious facilities for these institutions. All we call for are spaces that would bring dignity to tribal colleges and greater effectiveness to learning. For a college to be a respected part of the tribal and academic community, it requires good facilities. In addition, for students to be fully served, there must be—at the most basic level—adequate

74

classroom space and campus buildings that are aesthetically attractive and functional as well.

Third, we urge that connections between tribal colleges and non-Indian higher education be strengthened. Specifically, we recommend that four-year institutions work with tribal colleges for the transfer of credit and the development of cooperative degree payments. Many tribal colleges began with the support of other higher learning institutions. In the formative years of tribal colleges, non-Indian colleges offered courses, provided administrative support, and brought legitimacy to the tribal college movement. In some cases, this cooperation has continued and everyone has gained.

Turtle Mountain Community College, for example, began in the late 1960s when a group of young tribal members—calling themselves the Associates for Progress—invited colleges in the state to offer courses on the Turtle Mountain campus. In time, this fragmented series of programs was organized into a tribal educational center that existed under the aegis of a nearby campus of the North Dakota State University. By 1973, the enrichment center was recognized as Turtle Mountain Community College. It is now a fully tribally controlled institution.[2]

Similarly, the establishment of Fort Peck Community College in northeastern Montana was preceded by a series of courses offered on campus by Dawson Community College in 1969. The tribal college began nine years later under a bilateral agreement with another institution, Miles Community College.[3]

Standing Rock College in North Dakota began as a learning center affiliated with Bismarck Junior College, and in its early years, Oglala Lakota College in South Dakota developed agreements with a wide range of institutions, such as the University of Colorado, Black Hills State College, and the University of South Dakota.[4]

Collaboration has continued in many settings. By establishing a network of cooperative arrangements with colleges and universities in North Dakota for its new health services program, and a number of teacher education initiatives, Turtle Mountain has broadened its educational base. For many years, the University of North Dakota collaborated with Standing Rock College on a work-study degree program in elementary education that was strongly based on Sioux cultural traditions. The university also supported a wide range of Native American language programs at all four North Dakota tribal colleges.

Through its science program, Little Big Horn College has developed a close and cordial relationship with Montana State University. Selected as a research site for a federally funded bio-medical research program, Little Big Horn works closely with the state university, the recipient of the grant. The university provides Little Big Horn with funding for a federal researcher, student assistants, and necessary equipment. More important, however, this grant places Indian students in laboratories at the university's Bozeman, Montana campus and builds constructive connections between the two institutions.

According to Little Big Horn President Janine Pease-Windy Boy, students benefit through the hands-on experience in a field traditionally ignored by Native Americans. In addition, through work at the university campus, students are able to see that a broad range of educational opportunities exists outside of the reservation. Such cooperative projects help the tribal college to work as a more effective academic bridge to other institutions.

Faculty, too, are strengthened by an association which builds professional connections between instructors. "It creates avenues for our scientists to be colleagues with scientists at Montana State University," Windy Boy said. This is an otherwise difficult task for the small and isolated college.

Cooperation between these two institutions exists in other projects as well. Looking for additional ways to ease the often difficult transition from tribal college to state university, science instructor Robert Madsen tries to keep his courses compatible with those at Montana State. In some cases, Madsen follows the same texts and syllabi used at the university. This, he believes, better prepares students who plan to continue their studies at that institution.

For Montana State University's part, a tribal relations office has been created to work with tribal colleges statewide and coordinate joint projects. Hoping to increase cooperation between the institutions, President William Tietz even asked the university's vice presidents and deans to meet with members of the tribal college community in the state.

With connections at all levels, Little Big Horn—although small and not yet fully accredited—has benefited enormously. Faculty have grown professionally and students have been given both the opportunity and the skills necessary to succeed at a non-Indian college. As an example of the program's potential, a total of seven Little Big Horn students who have participated in the research program since its beginning in 1983 have successfully transferred to Montana State to continue their studies.

Montana State University has benefited, too. Through these innovative programs, faculty and administrators have gained an increased understanding of Native American issues, and Indian students who enter their institution from the tribal college are, as a result, more likely to succeed.

Not all students, however, enroll in a tribal college to complete a degree and then transfer. Those who *do* transfer to a non-Indian college are better prepared socially and academically for that experience. The Center for Native American Studies at Montana State University estimates that graduates from tribal colleges are at least twice as likely to succeed in a non-

Indian college as Indian students who did not first study at a tribally controlled institution.[5] This early evidence suggesting that tribal colleges can have a crucial impact is encouraging, since Indians traditionally have had among the highest non-completion rates of any college population.

It is also encouraging to note that several state college systems are working successfully with tribal colleges on a variety of transfer programs. But more needs to be done. Transfer is often dependent on the degree to which the tribal colleges use standard, discipline-oriented courses and standard textbooks. But their strength is in their distinctiveness—the ways they integrate cultural meanings with course material and view knowledge as interconnected. Such strengths need support.

Rather than viewing tribal colleges simply as institutions needing assistance, the non-Indian four-year colleges and universities should come to understand that they have much to learn about native culture and how to support native students more successfully.

On quite another front, Turtle Mountain is working with U.S. West, the region's telephone company, to offer programs in the health field. The college is creating cooperative arrangements with other area institutions for training in such professions as occupational therapy, nursing, and medical records. Students will complete a certificate degree through Turtle Mountain or be prepared to transfer elsewhere if a four-year degree is required. For its part, U.S. West is providing the support needed to study local needs, plan programs of study, and develop agreements with other colleges and universities.

Both Indian and non-Indian colleges are strengthened when they work together. Cooperative programs improve student education, promote faculty development, build bridges of understanding and, ultimately, result in students who have skills and confidence to work or continue their studies at non-Indian institutions.

78

Fourth, we recommend that programs linking tribal colleges to their communities be significantly increased. Every college is committed to responding to the tribe's economic and social needs. Salish Kootenai, for example, gives priority to job training through a work experience program. The college also offers in-service programs to educators and others throughout the reservation. Turtle Mountain Community College maintains close connections with tribally run industry. Sinte Gleska sponsors an institute to study the tribe's economic needs. Oglala Lakota works with the sponsoring tribe to support small-scale enterprises. Sinte Gleska also has a well developed literacy program, along with community education programs in alcohol and drug abuse that include a "Drug Free Schools" program funded through a Department of Education grant. Through such efforts, the impact of tribal colleges is felt by the entire tribe, demonstrating that Indians themselves can meet reservation needs.

Tribal college outreach also includes cooperation with schools that educate Indian children—public, tribal, and private. Such school-college collaboration recognizes that education and respect for native heritage and cultural experience must begin long before the students enter college. Oglala Lakota College has, for example, developed cooperative programs with such institutions as South Dakota State University, The Kennedy School of Government, and Hofstra University.

Several tribal colleges—such as Sinte Gleska and Standing Rock—have been directly responsible for increasing the number of Indian teachers in reservation schools.

Colleges can also promote the transition from school to college by offering classes that earn college credit. More directly, college students could receive credit for tutoring younger students in a variety of subjects. In turn, the colleges will be rewarded with students who are more firmly grounded in the basic skills and more confident of their abilities and self-identity. Tribal colleges, through such collaboration, affirm the fact that education is seamlessly connected to the community.

Fifth, we recommend that tribal colleges expand their important role of preserving the languages, history, and cultures of the tribes. The history of education for Native Americans in this country has been marked by the suppression of the rich heritage of the tribes. Textbooks have ignored the Indian traditions, sacred ceremonies have been ridiculed, and children have been punished if they spoke their native languages. One of the important missions of the tribal colleges is to preserve for Indians their great heritage, for purposes of identity, self-esteem, and cultural enrichment. Indian people need connections to those roots to survive physically and spiritually.

Maintenance of the native language and cultures also enriches *all* Americans. It brings us all back to the origins of this land we occupy.

James Shanley, president of Fort Peck Community College in Montana, concludes that "the native cultural heritage is a positive addition to the American experience. Without the preservation of the first culture," he says, "we can be assured that no other cultural traditions in this country will survive either." He concludes that "the United States will be all the poorer." While the federal government has contributed to cultural renewal through heritage grants and the bilingual education program, more attention needs to be paid to the work of preservation. In this regard, we recommend that foundations make available to tribal colleges special grants devoted specifically to the maintenance of Indian traditions.

Sixth, we recommend that state governments more adequately support tribal colleges. We urge especially that the states target funds for community service programs. A strong, self-supporting reservation benefits not only the members of the tribe, but the larger communities as well. In states

80

with large or multiple reservations, the economic and social health of the whole region can be greatly influenced by the status of these Indian communities.

Some reservations co-exist peacefully with the non-Indian population around them and maintain cordial relations with local and state governments. Indians do participate in surrounding economies, vote, and increasingly participate in local politics. In addition, growing numbers of Indian children are now being educated in public schools alongside non-Indian children.

In recent years, public schools serving the Flathead reservation of Montana and the Rosebud Sioux reservation of South Dakota have worked to teach all students an appreciation of local Indian culture. In Minnesota, the state university is actively involved in the development of Fond Du Lac Community College. And in North Dakota the state has cooperated with tribal colleges to develop Indian curricula for use in all schools.

Often, however, the mood of state government toward tribal colleges is less supportive, best described as an air of indifference. The needs of Native Americans frequently are not fully recognized by legislators. With limited economic power, and small to nonexistent political representation, Indian voices are rarely heard in the corridors of power. Policies affecting Indians, when they are considered by state agencies, often do not include adequate consultation. Thus, programs intended to benefit the Indian population may be ineffective or even counterproductive.

Tribally controlled colleges offer a splendid opportunity for legislatures to assist the reservations in their states. From the voting booth to government offices, communities benefit when Native Americans are educationally well prepared. In addition, tribal college programs in community development—from alcoholism to economic opportunity—benefit both Indian and surrounding Anglo society. When a tribe improves its own quality of life, the whole community is served.

We recommend, therefore, that state and local governments join with tribal colleges in partnerships for community development and educational excellence. An expanded cooperative effort between tribal colleges and government officials can improve the quality of education and the breadth of services at every college.

Seventh, we recommend the establishment of a comprehensive program for faculty development at tribal colleges. All colleges need programs to enrich faculty and build leadership at the administrative level. At tribal colleges, these needs are especially acute, since these institutions are young, operate under difficult conditions, and are often isolated. There is a strong need for foundations to support collaborative programs in support of leadership and faculty development at tribal colleges.

At the North and South Dakota tribal colleges, with their severely limited budgets and isolated locations, there is little opportunity for instructors to interact with peers. But with Bush Foundation support, these institutions have organized a variety of professional development programs. This is a workable model that could be replicated, we believe, at other colleges. During the three-year program, all vocational education teachers at Turtle Mountain, for example, became certified in their fields, and many other faculty have become active with their professional organizations.

Support from the Bush Foundation has increased professionalism on campuses, strengthened appreciation for native culture and, of equal importance, sparked discussion among the faculties at tribal institutions. The Bush faculty development programs have been productive and well received.

Another model is Little Big Horn's cooperation with Montana State University in biomedical research. It has been praised, not only for what it

82

offers students, but for how it builds connections between faculties at both schools. Projects such as these should be greatly expanded.

Eighth, we propose that foundations collaboratively support the Tribal College Institute, which is designed to strengthen administrative leadership in Native American higher education. Support for tribal college administrative leadership is crucial, too. Over the years, many tribal colleges have suffered from a high turnover rate among presidents and top administrators. New colleges, too, are often started by a cadre of people who are extremely dedicated to the cause of tribally controlled education, but may not have extensive administrative experience.

There is a need for presidents to work together to support common goals. All tribal colleges, for example, share similar educational, financial, and administrative challenges. While the overall structure varies greatly from campus to campus, all colleges share financial hardships and the broad goal of promoting education for Indian self-determination and tribal development. Programs and innovations found at one college can be meaningful to all colleges. From teaching methods to fund-raising options, tribal colleges have much to offer each other.

Restricted funds limit intercollegiate support. The presidents of tribal colleges do meet several times a year to discuss funding and legislative needs. They also get together once a year to hold small seminars during a week-long retreat. But the most valuable discussions—ones that could bring together a range of tribal college staff, administrators, instructors, and outside educators and policymakers—are simply not possible.

Most tribal colleges are members of the American Indian Higher Education Consortium. Together they provide guidance to new or struggling colleges, and also maintain a small Washington, D.C. office where Indian and education-oriented legislation is monitored. Recognizing that each

83

institution is part of the larger tribal college movement, as well as part of American higher education as a whole, tribal college administrators believe that much more must be done to develop intellectual and administrative leadership within their institutions.

Two new strategies have emerged, both of which hold great promise. First, the presidents of the consortium recently have organized a new continuing education program called the Tribal College Institute. Under the sponsorship of this organization, faculty and administrators from tribal colleges can meet regularly in seminars to discuss common needs and seek solutions to shared problems. The Institute is committed to building greater connections among tribally controlled colleges and between the colleges and the larger educational community. *We strongly urge that the Tribal College Institute be adequately supported. Foundations should provide funding for at least a five-year period.*

Tribal colleges have recently started a new journal called *Tribal College: Journal of American Indian Higher Education.* This publication will strengthen the network of institutions, provide for intellectual exchange, and give a sense of identity as well. The first issue provided a forum for both administrators and faculty, and in the future, this journal can be closely linked to Institute programs, providing a forum for Institute ideas. *Again, we urge that this project be supported during its initial five-year period.*

The achievement of the tribal colleges—as for any institution—is directly linked to the people they employ. Indeed, their creation and growth is testimony to the dedication and ability of college staff and faculty. For the colleges to grow and mature, the people associated with them also must grow in their professions. Along with its purpose of direct support to individual institutions, the Institute is, we believe, an important new way to provide this kind of enrichment and renewal.

Finally, if tribal colleges are to prosper, continuity of leadership is essential. Some presidents have successfully led their colleges for many years through a key developmental period. But future leaders must be developed within the Indian community. Here, too, the Tribal College Institute has a vital role to play as it brings together administrators with potential leaders from tribal colleges and other higher learning institutions.

Ninth, we recommend that the national awareness and advocacy programs for tribal colleges be strengthened. Specifically, we recommend that private philanthropies collaborate to provide, for three years, support for a Washington, D.C. office with a full-time director. Increased public awareness means better public policy, and there simply must be an increased understanding of the role tribal colleges play in the Native American communities and in society at large. As a group, these institutions are leaders in the movement for Indian self-determination and are increasingly responsible for encouraging large numbers of Indians to pursue higher education. In Montana, for example, the seven tribal colleges enroll more Native Americans than all of the state's other institutions combined. The same is true for the tribal colleges of North and South Dakota.

Most educators and policy-makers, however, do not even know these colleges exist. They have no idea that a network of tribal colleges plays an important role in Native American education or in community development. Nor do they recognize the increasingly significant role tribal colleges play in shaping the nation's American Indian policy.

The tribal colleges have organized themselves into a consortium with a part-time legislative representative in Washington, D.C. This organization must be strengthened. With such support, the colleges would enjoy the increased visibility needed to extend public awareness and heighten legislative understanding. In addition, the urgent need for comparative data on enrollment, growth, graduation and employment rates could be responded to by this central office. Until now, the colleges have had little time or money to complete this essential research at their own institutions. Yet, to argue their cases effectively, key information must be gathered in a professional and consistent manner.

Finally, we recommend that the newly established tribal college endowment be supported to increase the fiscal base and bring long-term stability to these institutions. On most tribal college campuses, budgets are tight and administrators are strained simply to provide basic academic and administrative services. Support from foundations, corporations, and federal funding agencies provide much-needed base support. Grants from these agencies help the colleges bridge the gap between merely existing and building a strong community of learning.

American higher education discovered long ago that quality cannot be achieved if an institution is forced to live from hand to mouth, with no stability in support. Endowments have become crucial in integrating long-range planning, cushioning unanticipated budget shortfalls, and increasing the stability of the institution. This is just as true for a new college as for our oldest and most prestigious institutions.

We urge, therefore, a major expansion of the endowment fund for the tribal colleges. Similar in intent to the United Negro College Fund, this endowment needs to benefit all member institutions. Further, Title III of the Tribal College Act provides for federal matching funds for endowment purposes. We urge that Congress commit itself to the building of long-term financial stability for tribal colleges through this important authorization.

Happily, in a consortium-wide effort, the Phelps Stokes Fund of New York is providing administrative and technical support for the development of the American Indian College Fund. While such money cannot replace

86

federal support, it can provide the margin of excellence, funding scholar-ships and specific development projects. The Phelps Stokes Fund should be commended for helping to nurture this still young and, to this point, modestly funded effort. We strongly recommend that foundations and other philanthropies make significant contributions to the American Indian College Fund.

During the Carnegie Foundation's two-year study of tribal colleges, we became convinced that the idea of Indian-controlled higher education is both valid and long overdue. We also concluded that the growing network of tribally controlled colleges offers great hope to the Native American com-munity and the nation as a whole.

At the same time, we saw problems. Tribal colleges have distressingly inadequate facilities, poor salaries, understaffed academic programs, and frequently they encounter divisive politics. Graduation, continued educa-tion, and employment rates are not well documented. The need for sound research is urgent. All of this was noted in our visits.

As a movement, however, tribal colleges are an inspiration. These institutions are creating opportunity for Native Americans who, for more than three hundred years, suffered shameful misunderstanding and abuse. Tribal colleges offer hope. They can, with adequate support, continue to open doors of opportunity to the coming generations and help Native American communities bring together a cohesive society, one that draws inspiration from the past in order to shape a creative, inspired vision of the future.

Tribally Controlled Colleges

BAY MILLS COMMUNITY COLLEGE
Ms. Martha McLeod, President
Rt. 1
Brimley, Michigan 49715

BLACKFEET COMMUNITY COLLEGE
Mr. Gordon Belcourt, President
P.O. Box 819
Browning, Montana 59417

CHEYENNE RIVER COMMUNITY COLLEGE
Ms. A. Gay Kingman, President
P.O. Box 220
Eagle Butte, South Dakota 57625

CROWNPOINT INSTITUTE OF TECHNOLOGY
Mr. James Tutt, President
P.O. Box Drawer K
Crownpoint, New Mexico 87313

D-Q UNIVERSITY
Mr. Carlos Cordero, President
P.O. Box 409
Davis, California 95617

DULL KNIFE MEMORIAL COLLEGE
Dr. Art McDonald, President
P.O. Box 98
Lame Deer, Montana 59043

FOND DU LAC COMMUNITY COLLEGE
Dr. Jack Briggs, President
105 University Road
Cloquet, Minnesota 55720

FORT BELKNAP COMMUNITY COLLEGE
Ms. Margaret Perez, President
P.O. Box 547
Harlem, Montana 59526

FORT BERTHOLD COLLEGE
Ms. Phyllis Howard, President
P.O. Box 490
New Town, North Dakota 58763

FORT PECK COMMUNITY COLLEGE
Dr. James Shanley, President
P.O. Box 575
Poplar, Montana 59255

LAC COURTE OREILLES
OJIBWA COMMUNITY COLLEGE
Dr. Jasjit Minhas, President
R.R. 2, Box 2357
Hayward, Wisconsin 54843

LITTLE BIG HORN COLLEGE
Ms. Janine Pease-Windy Boy, President
P.O. Box 370
Crow Agency, Montana 59022

LITTLE HOOP COMMUNITY COLLEGE
Dr. Merril Berg, President
P.O. Box 269
Fort Totten, North Dakota 58335

NAVAJO COMMUNITY COLLEGE
Mr. Lawrence Gishey, President
c/o Navajo Community College
Tsaile, Arizona 86556

NEBRASKA INDIAN COMMUNITY COLLEGE
Ms. Thelma Thomas, President
P.O. Box 752
Winnebago, Nebraska 68071

NORTHWEST INDIAN COLLEGE
Dr. Robert J. Lorence, President
2522 Kwina Road
Bellingham, Washington 98226

OGLALA LAKOTA COLLEGE
Dr. Lowell Amiotte, President
P.O. Box 490
Kyle, South Dakota 57752

SALISH KOOTENAI COLLEGE
Dr. Joseph McDonald, President
P.O. Box 117
Pablo, Montana 59855

SINTE GLESKA COLLEGE
Mr. Lionel Bordeaux, President
P.O. Box 490
Rosebud, South Dakota 57570

SISSETON-WAHPETON COMMUNITY COLLEGE
Ms. Gwen Hill, President
Agency Village, P.O. Box 689
Sisseton, South Dakota 57262

STANDING ROCK COLLEGE
Dr. David Archambault, President
P.O. Box 450
Fort Yates, North Dakota 58538

STONE CHILD COLLEGE
Ms. Peggy Nagel, President
Rocky Boy Route, Box 1082
Box Elder, Montana 59521

TURTLE MOUNTAIN COMMUNITY COLLEGE
Mr. Gerald Monette, President
P.O. Box 340
Belcourt, North Dakota 58316

UNITED TRIBES TECHNICAL COLLEGE
Mr. David Gipp, President
3315 University Drive
Bismarck, North Dakota 58501

NOTES

CHAPTER 1

1. Patricia Porter McNamara, *American Indians in U.S. Higher Education* (Los Angeles: Higher Education Research Institute, 1984), p. 104.

CHAPTER 2

1. Alice C. Fletcher, *Indian Education and Civilization: A Report Prepared in Answer to Senate Resolution of February 23, 1885* (Washington, D.C.: Government Printing Office, 1888), pp. 32–33.

2. Ibid., p. 33.

3. Ibid., p. 53.

4. Ibid., p. 54.

5. Ibid.

6. Francis Paul Prucha, *The Indians in American Society From the Revolutionary War to the Present* (Berkeley: Univ. of California Press, 1985), pp. 6–8.

7. Ibid., p. 6.

8. Ibid., p. 12.

9. Benjamin Franklin, *Two Tracts, Information to Those Who Would Remove to America and Remarks Concerning the Savages of North America,* 3rd ed. (London: 1794) pp. 28–29; cited in Estelle Fuchs and

Robert Havighurst, *To Live on This Earth: American Indian Education* (Garden City, N.Y.: Doubleday, 1973), p. 3.

10. Frederick Law Olmsted, *A Journey Through Texas* (1857; reprint, with foreword by Larry McMurtry, Austin: Univ. of Texas Press, 1978), pp. 289–90.

11. Charles Maclaren, *Werner Encyclopedia,* vol. I, pp. 602, 604; cited in *The Indian in America's Past,* ed. J. Forbes (Englewood Cliffs, N. J.: Prentice-Hall, 1964), p. 17.

12. Richard Henry Pratt, *Battlefield and Classroom: Four Decades with the American Indian, 1867–1904,* ed. and with an introduction by Robert M. Utley (Lincoln: Univ. of Nebraska Press, 1987), p. 335.

13. Elaine Eastman, *Pratt: The Red Man's Moses* (Norman: Univ. of Oklahoma, 1935), p. 85.

14. Ibid.

15. Ida S. Patterson, *Montana Memories: The Life of Emma Magee in the Rocky Mountain West, 1866–1950* (Pablo, Mont.: Salish Kootenai Community College, 1981), pp. 90–91.

16. *Tentative Course of Study for United States Indian Schools* (Washington, D.C.: Government Printing Office, 1915), p. 5.

17. Francis Paul Prucha, *Americanizing the American Indian* (Cambridge: Harvard Univ. Press, 1973), pp. 257–59.

18. Margaret Connell Szasz, *Education and the American Indian: The Road to Self-Determination Since 1928* (Albuquerque: Univ. of New Mexico Press, 1974), p. 10.

19. Prucha, *The Indians in American Society,* p. 51.

20. Lewis Meriam, *The Problem of Indian Administration* (Baltimore: Johns Hopkins Press, 1928), pp. 3–5.

21. *New York Times*, 23 May 1928.

22. Meriam, p. 32.

23. "The Right To Be An Indian," *New York Times*, 2 Dec. 1928.

24. John Collier, *Indians of the Americas*, abridged (New York: Mentor, 1947), p. 155.

25. Ibid.

26. Szasz, p. 78.

CHAPTER 3

1. Steven Crum, "The Idea of an Indian College or University in Twentieth Century America Before the Formation of the Navajo Community College in 1968," *Tribal College: Journal of American Indian Higher Education*, vol. 1, (Summer 1989): p. 20.

2. August Breuninger, to Dr. Carlos Montezuma, 2 Mar. 1911, Carlos Montezuma papers (State Historical Society of Wisconsin, 1975, microfilm ed.), p. 20.

3. Susan Guyette and Charlotte Heth, *Issues for the Future of American Indian Studies*, UCLA, 1985.

4. Fort Berthold Community College, *A Report for an Evaluation for Continued Candidacy*, 1985, p. 46.

5. Little Hoop Community College, *Self Study*, no date, pp. 13–14.

6. Standing Rock College, *Self Study*, no date, pp. 3–4.

7. Turtle Mountain Community College, *Self Study*, 1984, p. 21.

CHAPTER 4

1. Jon Reyhner, "Indian Teachers as Cultural Translators." *Journal of American Indian Higher Education,* (November, 1981): p. 22.

2. "Chief Wilma Mankiller Helps Cherokees Build Pride," *U.S. News and World Report,* 17 Feb. 1986, p. 64.

3. "The Killing Fields of Rosebud," *U.S. News and World Report,* 2 Sept. 1985.

4. James Cook, "A New Style of Indian Giving," *Forbes,* 20 May 1985, p. 154.

CHAPTER 5

1. Robert N. Bellah, et al., *Habits of the Heart: Individualism and Commitment in American Life* (Berkeley: Univ. of California Press, 1985), pp. 281–82.

2. Jack Forbes, *Native American Higher Education: The Struggle for the Creation of D-Q University, 1960–1971* (Davis, Cal.: D-Q Univ. Press, 1985), p. 47.

3. Danielle Sanders, "Cultural Conflicts: An Important Factor in the Academic Failure of American Indian Students," *Journal of Multicultural Counseling and Development* (April 1987): p. 85.

4. Herbert John Benally, "Dine Bo'ohoo'aah Bindii'a: Navajo Philosophy of Learning," *Dine Be'iina': A Journal of Navajo Life* (Spring 1987): pp. 141–43.

5. Ibid., pp. 145–47.

6. McNamara, p. 75.

7. Ibid., p. 90.

8. Sinte Gleska College, *Self Study Report,* 1987, pp. 96, 102.

9. Tom Allen, of Oglala Lakota College, staff communication, 13 Sept. 1989.

10. Art McDonald, of Dull Knife Memorial College, staff communication, 12 Sept. 1989.

11. Gwen Hill, of Sisseton-Wahpeton Community College, staff communication, 12 Sept. 1989.

12. Turtle Mountain Community College, *Self Study,* 1984, p. 31.

13. Standing Rock College, *Self Study,* 1987, pp. 84–85.

14. Tom Allen, ibid.

15. *Building Communities: A Vision for a New Century,* a report of the Commission on the Future of Community Colleges, American Association of Community and Junior Colleges, 1988.

CHAPTER 6

1. U.S. Congress, Senate Hearings Before the Select Committee on Indian Affairs, 20 March 1986, p. 1.

2. Wayne Stein, *A History of Tribally Controlled Community Colleges: 1968–1978* (Ph.D. diss., Washington State Univ.), pp. 137–43.

3. Ibid., p. 218.

4. Ibid., pp. 85–98, 164.

5. Bobby Wright, "An Assessment of Student Outcomes at Tribally Controlled Community Colleges," paper presented at the 18th Annual National Indian Education Association Conference, 22 Nov. 1986, p. 12.

INDEX

Tribal government, 18, 19, 21; and
    impact of economic development,
    49; termination of, 20
Tribally Controlled Community
    College Assistance Act (1978), 24,
    36, 70, 74, 86
Turtle Mountain Community College,
    60, 61; Associates for Progress, 75;
    curriculum, 28, 56, 57, 78; economic
    development program, 64–65, 79;
    faculty development, 82; High
    school equivalency exam, 63;
    physical facilities, 34; students, 31
Turtle Mountain Manufacturing, 65
Turtle Mountain Reservation, 43, 59;
    and Bureau of Indian Affairs, 72
Tutoring programs, 3, 62, 79

United Negro College Fund, 86
United States government, and
    Indian cultural renewal, 80; and
    support for Indian education, 69–
    72; and suppression of Indian
    culture, 7–21, 39; Bureau of Indian
    Affairs, 19, 20, 41, 49, 71–72;
    Department of Education, 79;
    Forest Service, 43; funding of tribal
    colleges, 35, 36, 69–72; general
    policies; 1, 15, 39, 40; Indian
    attitudes towards, 25;

recommendations for action by, 69–
    75
University of Colorado, 75
University of Maine, 47
University of North Dakota, 76
University of South Dakota, 75
U.S. West (telephone company), 78

Values, Indian, 42, 55; cooperation,
    57; and education, 4; family, 45, 46;
    forgiveness, 56
Vocational education, 4, 11, 14, 17,
    28; faculty development, 82; Carl
    Perkins Vocational Education
    Grant, 70–71
Volunteer programs, 29, 62, 64
Voting: *See* Political participation

Walking Bull, Loraine, 62–63
Wars with Indians, 10–11
White Hat, Albert, 42, 53
William and Mary, College of, 8
Wilkie, Emma, 57
Windy Boy: *see* Pease-Windy Boy,
    Janine
Woodcock, Clarence, 43
Work/study programs, 76
World War II, effect on teacher
    training, 19